CONTENTS

Contents

Everyday Dharma

Everyday Dharma

Seven Weeks to Finding the Buddha in You

Lama Willa Miller

QUEST
BOOKS

Theosophical Publishing House
Wheaton, Illinois * Chennai, India

Quest Books
Theosophical Publishing House
P. O. Box 270
Wheaton, IL 60187-0270

www.questbooks.net

Cover image by Trinette Reed/Getty Images
Cover design by Kirsten Hansen Pott

Library of Congress Cataloging-in-Publication Data

Miller, Willa.
Everyday dharma: seven weeks to finding the buddha in you / Lama
Willa Miller.
  p. cm.
Includes index.
ISBN 978-0-8356-0883-1
1. Spiritual life—Buddhism.   I. Title.
BQ5660.M54 2009
294.3'444—dc22   2009014452

5   4   3   2   1   *   09   10   11   12   13   14

Printed in the United States of America

This book is dedicated to the Sage in you.

Truth is what stands the test of experience.
                                    —Albert Einstein

To see things in the seed is genius.
                                    —Lao Tzu

Acknowledgments

From the point of view of the Buddha's teachings on interdependence, acknowledgments are due to every living being, and from the point of view of a spiritual practitioner, gratitude should be boundless. So the following is just a tiny portion of the thanks due to the many people who have helped contribute to this book directly and indirectly.

Dharma students, friends, and family members contributed to this project indirectly by asking many good questions and nudging me in the direction of simplification—for them I am thankful.

I am deeply grateful to my literary agent, John White, for catching on to the book's vision from the beginning.

I would like to thank from my heart the people who read and commented on the manuscript for *Everyday Dharma* in its various versions: John Makransky, Lama Surya Das, Leah Weiss, Jane Moss, Julie Forsythe, John and Linda Dean, and Jill Stockwell. I am especially indebted to those at Quest Books who helped make the book a reality: publishing manager Sharron Dorr, publicist Xochi Adame, and editors Richard Smoley and Judith Stein, whose comments throughout made this a better book and who offered support, advice, and encouragement during the editing process.

A deep bow of gratitude to my root teachers who are the contributors behind the book: Kalu Rinpoche, Dilgo Khentse Rinpoche, Bokar Rinpoche, Lama Norlha Rinpoche, and Khenpo Tsultrim Gyatso Rinpoche. I would also like to extend sincere thanks to Lama Palden Drolma of the Sukhasiddhi Foundation for her inspirational example, and to my husband, Mike, for his loving and loyal support.

Introduction

One isn't necessarily born with courage, but one is born with potential.

—Maya Angelou

"Buddhas—are they made or born?"

I was sitting at the feet of a Buddhist lama in a Tibetan refugee camp with my little list of handwritten questions. I might have written at the top, "Riddles to Stump the Lamas." I carried this list around with me from robed priest to robed priest in my early days as the skeptical college seeker, imagining that eventually my questions about the meaning of life would resolve themselves through contact with great Eastern thinkers.

"Made . . . and born," the lama replied. I wondered if this wise master was playfully withholding an explanation—or did he mean it?

"How can a buddha be made and born at the same time?"

"From the point of view of who we really are, buddhas are born. But from the point of view of a spiritual path, buddhas are made."

I was nineteen and living in a tiny refugee camp nestled in the northern Himalayan range in Nepal. It was worlds away from the groomed lawns and genteel classrooms of Vassar, where the rest of my friends were attending lectures on art history and reading Kant. At the moment, that world left behind seemed weirdly alien to me, and the mud-floored one-room adobe hut where I slept on cotton batting and cooked on a camp stove felt like home. This was the classroom I wanted to be in. I wondered if I had been born on the wrong continent.

The lama, my source of spiritual wisdom at that time, lived quietly in a tiny monk's cell overlooking the courtyard of the village monastery. I can still see his wrinkled face, lined like folded raw silk, and his long gray beard against the backdrop of the square of blue Himalayan sky that was his window.

What was the lama trying to tell me? Later, I learned that *buddha* means "one who is awake" and refers to a person whose wisdom and compassion has fully blossomed or awakened—a person of a very high order, a sage. However, paradoxically, buddha lives in every one of us, as the *potential* to wake up to wisdom and compassion. We are all born with an inner sage. That is why, on the one hand, we are born buddhas, but—on the other hand—we still need to *become* buddhas: we still need to wake up to the wisdom and compassion sleeping in our deepest being. That moment in the refugee camp was a wake-up call for me, so to speak. It was the first time I had an inkling that while I might have many small missions in life—to finish school, to spend time with my friends, to travel—there was one big mission that should not be missed: to wake up to inner wisdom and compassion. Even if that took a long time, it was a goal worth holding onto.

Everyday Dharma

The bridge of *becoming*, the bridge between pure potential and its actualization, is not built in a day, at least not for most of us. It is built gradually, over the years, through everyday spiritual practice. It is built by consciously observing your mind and actions and then doing the physical, psychological, and spiritual work to move closer to your wisdom-nature. It is built on experimentation and experience. I believe that waking up is not a quick fix; it is a process—and a fluid process at that.

The word *dharma* comes from the Sanskrit root *dhr*, which means "to uphold." The word in Hindu and Buddhist texts has many meanings, from "phenomena" to "highest truth." One of its meanings is simply "duty," in the sense of an obligation to yourself or to your community, an obligation to uphold the common good. This gets closer to how I will be using the term *dharma* in this book—to mean spiritual practice. Dharma is what you do, what you practice, every day to make your mind, and your world, a better place to live. To practice dharma means to create and sustain a commitment to becoming more awake and aware, to becoming wiser and more loving, and to discovering one's wisdom-nature. But dharma is more than commitment. It is action: it is the action you take to unearth your inner buddha (or Jesus or Mary or Shiva or fill-in-your-blank) and to become wiser and more compassionate. If wisdom were a destination, dharma—played out in our thoughts and actions—is the path leading there. Dharma is the art of living a wise and compassionate life.

The Compassionate Sage

For many people, the words *wisdom* and *sage* evoke images of stoic detachment, or—perhaps more flatteringly—a sense of knowledge garnered through experience, or an unflappable calm. I wonder what it is about our culture that has evolved a language for sagacious perfection that is so "in the head." In Buddhist understanding, perfect wisdom is rooted in the heart, in love and compassion. In Buddhist texts, the same word is used for "heart" and "mind." The seat of love *is* the seat of knowledge. And, conversely, where there is real wisdom, there must be love.

So the path of dharma is a path with a heart—the Buddhist notion of dharma is warm to the core. In Buddhist sources, a person who follows such a love-wisdom path is called a *bodhisattva*. The word *bodhisattva* literally means "awakening one." A bodhisattva is a person who is on a quest to wake up, or stimulate, his or her love and wisdom. Buddhist texts are full of stories of bodhisattvas. Sometimes they are save-the-world types who make extraordinary sacrifices on behalf of others. Sometimes they are quiet recluses whose small acts of kindness extend even to animals, insects, and birds. Sometimes they are teachers. Sometimes they are children. Sometimes they are animals. Whatever the circumstances may be, such bodhisattvas are spiritual heroes.

In this book, I have settled on the term *sage* to translate *bodhisattva*. It may not be literal, but it captures the essence of a being who exists to

Dharma Tip

In the Buddhist tradition, a central goal of a spiritual seeker is to train as a bodhisattva. *Bodhi* means "awakening" or "enlightenment." *Sattva* means "one who exists." So a bodhisattva is one who exists in order to awaken. This does not refer to waking up from a good night's sleep, but rather waking up from the sleep of ignorance and apathy into the daylight of wisdom and compassion. Such a person's purpose in life is to wake up his or her potential for the highest good and to express this awakening as conscious acts of kindness. Therefore, a bodhisattva, or *"one who exists to awaken,"* is both kind and wise.

develop wisdom, who lives to wake up. The word *sage* comes from the Latin word *sapius*, meaning "taste" or "experience." The compassionate bodhisattva, the sage envisioned in this book, is a taster and an experiencer. What does that mean? To be a sage is to value experience as the primary path to wisdom, rather than valuing the acquisition of knowledge solely from the outside. If we wish to develop wisdom, we must learn from experience, long to taste the truth directly, and not be satisfied with hearsay. We must embrace the world of the senses rather than running from it, using sight, sound, touch, taste, and feeling as doors to wisdom. The path of the sage is a path of developing inner senses as well, a keen ability to taste—to know and assess—with the mind and the heart. We sharpen our inner senses through meditation and contemplation. Everyday dharma, therefore, is a path of outer and inner tasting. It is both an empirical path and an intuitive path. Dharma is a path of inner and outer experience.

A Proviso

Many people think that Tibetan Buddhism is a single tradition, but that is not the case. Just as with "American Christianity" or "British Judaism" or "Iranian Islam," the label covers many subgroups. This book borrows from the tools of the Tibetan Buddhist tradition, but it should not be taken as an orthodox or normative representation of the Tibetan Buddhist perspective. My intent is to adapt Tibetan Buddhist techniques for a Western audience interested in personal transformation. It also reflects how I have used and understood the teachings in my own life and work.

Many new students of spirituality and Buddhism do not initially have contact with a teacher. They start with books, so it seems to me there should be books available that show people how to start a practice. I notice that students who have already started to read and practice on their own tend to relate to "live" teachings more easily than those who have not initially explored meditation on their own through books. These students in some way have already tried on the ideas and practices.

The Next Seven Weeks

You do not have to subscribe to a belief system to benefit from the material in this book. In my own life, I have met Christians, Muslims, Jews, Hindus, Wiccans, Unitarians, and agnostics who use the tools of meditation and conventional wisdom offered in Buddhist sources. There is no corner on the market for becoming a better person or awakening authentic wisdom. It is, or should be, free to those who seek it.

This book is intended as a spiritual manual to be read over the next seven weeks. Those seven weeks might be the beginning of your spiritual journey; or, if you are already on a spiritual path, this book may serve as an enhancement of that path. No matter what your background is, I hope this book will be more than just informative; I hope it will also be useful. Over the course of the next seven weeks, *Everyday Dharma* can help you sketch an outline of what a meaningful life looks like for you. It will challenge you to see your life as an adventure. It may change where you look for answers. You may discover that the answers to the deepest questions you have about life cannot be provided by a book or a person. You may find that while a book or person can make suggestions, the real answers are within you.

Introduction

In Tibetan, one word for enlightenment is *tarpa*, which means "freedom." In one sense, tarpa implies freedom *from* something: from negative habitual patterns and ignorance. In another sense, tarpa means the freeing *of* something. It is the freeing of a true nature that is fully a part of each of us. The practice of this spiritual path involves freeing up your authentic true nature, your innate purity, your buddha-nature, or (in the words that I will use in this book) your wisdom-nature so that it can shine out into your life and the world.

This Is Your Manual

A book is a forum for interaction, so you should interact with this book. Question. Wonder. Write in the margins. Underline. Highlight. Do what you need to make it useful to you. Make this book a part of your personal adventure. Why be a passive recipient of its contents?

Everyday Dharma is divided into seven chapters, one for each of the next seven weeks of your life. For this book really to serve its purpose, it is best to read it slowly and take the full seven weeks to complete it. The truth is that most of the practices in this book could take more than one lifetime to perfect, so there is no rush from that perspective! The most meaningful and lasting changes in life take time.

The techniques in this book draw on ancient methods of a tradition that has been time-tested for thousands of years. These methods were designed to bring about spiritual evolution in the person who practices them, and it has been my experience that they work. They work best when repeated over months and years, when practiced consistently, but they work to some degree the first time you try them. Each chapter is divided into seven days. Each day provides you with:

A passage to read. The passages in the book are laid out in a day-by-day format. At the beginning of each day's passage, record the date in the place provided. This will allow you to keep track of your process through the book. Missing or skipping a day is not a problem. Reading just a bit each day gives you time to let the material sink in.

An exercise. This is something for you to do that relates to the week's topic. Sometimes an exercise is as simple as thinking and writing something down. Sometimes the exercise is a contemplation or meditation. The exercises in this book are designed to turn your reading into dharma, to bring your inner journey into the world in some way. We can talk about "spiritual development," but if our inner work does not change how we live, love, interact, and so forth, it is not really dharma.

A quotation. In the East, religious people often memorize quotations for inspiration. Sages are all around us, so I have drawn not just from Buddhist sources but from many sources of wisdom. Every day of the week the book provides a quotation to consider. Cut out or copy down the ones you like. Take them to work, school, or wherever you spend your day. Do not just accept a quotation's contents. Try it on for size. Use it as a koan, an enigma to chew on. Examine whether and how it applies to your life. Ask yourself if you find it to be true and useful. Why or why not?

Dharma Tip

Each day of your spiritual journey, there are just three steps to complete: Record the date, read the pages for the day, and do the exercise for that day. Take your time, and move through the course day by day. Savor the journey!

Dharma tips. Occasionally, you will find Dharma Tips. These provide a little more detail where detail is needed and are designed to make your daily practice a bit easier.

Reading This Book with a Friend

Reading this book with a friend, several friends, or a dharma buddy is a powerful way to move through your seven-week course. Friends can help each other by creating a circle of interaction. They provide more insights than we may have by ourselves. So why not find a friend with interests similar to yours with whom to read this book? Try meeting weekly and using the exercises and reading passages for discussion points. (I have created a Facebook page for people to connect with each other on the Internet at http://www.facebook.com/group.php?gid=66456785488.)

Another way to commune with a friend using this book is to do the meditation or contemplation exercises together. I first began Buddhist meditation using a book on Zen meditation by Aitken Roshi. I remember enjoying the process of sitting down with the book and following his meditation advice. But part of me wished that I had someone there to practice with. I envisioned reading the instructions to my friend while he or she meditated, and vice versa. This is what you can do with your reading partner. A friend is a good support for meditation. But to develop some independence, sometimes do the meditations on your own. Learning to meditate alone is also a skill worth cultivating, since your friend might not be around every moment of every day!

Dharma Tip

Contemplation and meditation are different activities. Contemplation is a process of sitting quietly and deeply probing a topic to better understand it. Meditation involves greater focus and concentration and is less discursive than contemplation. The intent of meditation is to calm the mind and body and ultimately to experience the authentic being, or wisdom-nature, that we each have. The contemplations and meditations described here are central to getting the most out of this book. Once you have tried a contemplation or meditation, you can stick with it daily if you like until you receive the one for the following week.

Getting Started

How often do you wake up excited to face the day? My hope for you, as you go through Week One, is that you will begin to reclaim the excitement about life that is due you. Why is it due you? The process of creating a spiritual life is largely a process of discovering that you deserve to be happy. You deserve to live a fulfilling and meaningful life. You deserve to bring your innate wisdom-nature to its full blossoming.

For me, the experience of following a spiritual path is a little like falling in love every day. When you are in love, the beloved's presence colors every experience. He or she is the first thing you think of when you wake up and the last thing you think of before sleep. It is possible to relate to the spiritual path in that way, as a joyful presence. Like the beloved, it puts the color in the cinema of life. It makes your life an adventure. Like a lover, you can wake up every day, not just ready to meet the day, but excited to meet it.

When I first started out on the long road of the spiritual apprentice, I was eager and energized about what I was learning, but I did not know what actually to do. There were so many practices, so many traditions, so many foreign words, and it all seemed so complicated. It was almost impossible to sort out what was essential from what was superfluous. I needed a guide. I needed some inspiration. I found it in bits and pieces at first, but it was years until I found an organized curriculum and a way in which to become immersed.

This is the kind of handbook I wish I had had in those early days. My gift to you is the handbook that I never had. This is the start of your spiritual journey, of discovering within the sage that you really are.

Are you ready? Let us begin.

The Zen "genius" sleeps in every one of us and demands an awakening.

—D. T. Suzuki, twentieth-century Zen Master

Week One

Know Your Potential

Step one of your spiritual journey is to discover that you have the potential to awaken to your innate wisdom-nature.

*F*ew people have confidence when they first set foot on the spiritual path, and even fewer sustain that confidence when the going gets rocky. Few of us realize—in a sustained way—the power of our inborn spiritual potential.

One of my favorite stories about spiritual potential was told to me by a weathered old Tibetan nomad on the high-altitude tundra of central Tibet. As we sipped hot butter-tea, the nomad spun his tale, which he called "The Farmer and the Yogi." It goes like this:

In Tibet, there lived a barley farmer. One day he heard a rumor that a yogi had moved into a rocky cave in the mountain behind his farm. The farmer knew a bit about yogis. They were reclusive figures living in high mountain sanctuaries who devoted their lives to meditation, prayer, and rigorous spiritual practice. He had heard monks speak with admiration of the yogis' meditation abilities. He overheard women spinning tales of their miraculous powers. As a child, he had seen his mother give alms to a man in a brown cotton robe with mounds of hair piled high on his head—a yogi, he would later learn. But the farmer himself had never spoken to one.

The farmer's curiosity got the better of him, and he hiked up the mountainside to the yogi's cave. In the shadow of a rock overhang, the farmer saw the yogi deeply absorbed in meditation. Other than a cooking pot, a sleeping mat, and a small bag of barley flour, he had no worldly possessions. The farmer was impressed and inspired by this ascetic's dedication to the spiritual life. Not wanting to disturb him, the farmer went back down to his farm to gather milk, yogurt, rock candy, and barley flour to offer the hermit as sustenance. He continued with these offerings every few days.

Some time later, it occurred to the farmer, *I should really request a teaching from this great man. Maybe I, too, can follow a spiritual path.*

So the next day, when he brought a bag of barley, he asked, "Master, would you please give me a teaching? I would like to learn something about the spiritual path. Please accept me as your disciple."

"If you want to understand the path, you should go on a pilgrimage," replied the yogi.

"But I was hoping you could give me a teaching," insisted the farmer.

"If you want a teaching," said the yogi, "go to the Lake of the Goddess's Soul in the south. It is a magical lake—the eye of the goddess! You will see the Buddha in the lake. No teaching I can give is better than that!"

"I will!" replied the farmer excitedly, saying to himself, *the teacher must think I am special to give such a prophesy!* "How long should I wait for the vision?"

"You will only need to stay a day. You will have a vision the first day," the yogi promised.

The farmer eagerly packed up his belongings and set out on the long, arduous journey to the Lake of the Goddess's Soul. When he reached the lake's edge, he sat down and stared into the deep blue of the lake. He waited and waited. At the end of the day, he had seen nothing unusual in the lake. Even so, he stayed an extra day just in case. Still he saw nothing but what one would expect—some floating leaves, some stones, surface reflections. Disappointed, he returned to his barley farm. The next day, he climbed wearily up the mountain to report his failed attempt at a vision to his teacher. When he got to the top, the yogi was outside his cave basking in the early, high-altitude sunshine.

"I went to the lake and waited for the vision of the Buddha. But I did not see anything at all," the farmer said sheepishly.

"Nothing?" asked the yogi.

"Nothing but some leaves, some stones—oh, and my reflection."

"Ah, then you did see the Buddha." The yogi's eyes twinkled. "You saw the Buddha precisely."

Day One

Wisdom-Nature

If daily you observe the mind-jewel, the innate nature shining forth, you know how things really are—others may speak of it, but what do they know?

—Kanha

Today's Date: _____

The story about the yogi and the farmer is an old allegory for the seeker's journey. Does it sound at all familiar? Like the farmer on his pilgrimage for wisdom, we all have goals, aspirations, and visions that we dream to achieve. The farmer hoped for a vision of the Buddha. We desire a vision of spiritual truth, happiness, and a meaningful life, and we long for fulfillment of our dreams of success, wealth, and contentment.

Like the farmer, we are sojourners. We are pilgrims. And, like the farmer, we are likely—at some point or other—to encounter a profound irony of our spiritual journey. The spiritual seeker's irony, the cosmic joke on all of us who plod through the jungle of mystical traditions, is this: Whatever we have been seeking has been with us all along, like the farmer's reflection in the lake. Like the farmer's vision of the Buddha, spirituality—inner purity, wisdom, whatever we want to call it—eludes us until we discover the real Buddha, or God, or Shiva, or Shakti, or Jesus, or Mary, or Muhammad reflected in ourselves. Then, and only then, we get the moral of our own life story: We are, in essence, pure at heart. We are, in essence, Buddha. Or, to put it in other words, we are not on our way to becoming a sage. At some level, in the deepest part of our being, we already are.

Week One

Wisdom traditions around the world give many names to the innate but inchoate perfection of our spirit, the wisdom-nature, the spiritual genius that lives in every person: the soul, God, basic goodness, Krishna consciousness, Atman, the inner light. It is waiting to be purified, saved, developed, awakened, or sometimes just noticed, depending on the tradition. Buddhists throughout the ages have called it the highest potential, the basic heart of awakening, buddha-nature, the Element, the awakening mind, the spiritual gene, and the seed of enlightenment. All these epithets are translations of Sanskrit or Pali terms. Just as the Inuit language has many words for snow, Buddhists over the ages have produced many words for our inner spiritual genius. This is lucky for us. The more synonyms provided by these profound texts, the more handles we have for grasping an intangible concept like spiritual potential.

In this book, I will refer to this concept as "wisdom-nature." This is merely a translation of the Sanskrit term *tathagatha-garbha*. A slightly more literal translation is "the seed of the Transcendent One." The Transcendent One is just another name for the Buddha and refers to the fact that a *buddha*—any awakened, enlightened being—is one who has *transcended limiting states of ignorance, aversion, and desire, and gone to wisdom*. So, to put it together, your wisdom-nature is the seed of your transcendence. It is your potential to blossom into a loving person, a sage, a community leader, a wise example—to become a hero in your family and your community. Your wisdom-nature is the heart of who you are spiritually.

That does not mean you have to be religious, or spiritual in any mystical sense, to envision and trust the wisdom-nature at the core of your being. This Buddhist teacher, for one, admits to being a "religious erratic" some of the time (the alter ego, I suppose, of a religious fanatic). Some of the time I am fielding the questions of the inner dissident: *Hey, wait a minute! How does this fit in with genetics, natural selection, medicine, psychology, string theory?* I am always delighted to hear someone come up with another definition of this potential: the genetic predisposition to altruism, the urge to uncover truth, the transpersonal space, a tendency to social justice. . . . Whatever you define as the most courageous, sacred, selfless, and transcendent part or parts of yourself can be viewed as the expression of your wisdom-nature. There is a great sense of empowerment that comes from beginning to define and value your most authentic nature, the deepest part of your being, or your strongest potential for good.

About the wisdom-nature, the Buddha said, "No mistake can ruin it, and no virtue can make it any better." Because this most sacred part of you exists as an innate seed or predisposition, your wisdom-nature is unaffected by who you are or what you may have done in life. It does not matter if you are a man or a woman. It does not matter how old you are or where you come from. It does not matter what color your skin is or what physical condition you are in. It does not matter what mistakes you have made or what tragedies have befallen you. It does not matter what you think of yourself or others. It does not even matter what species you are. Wisdom-nature is the birthright of every person, even every living creature. It is your deepest self and your brightest promise. By virtue of having that wisdom-nature, you are a sage at heart already.

But if we each have a wisdom-nature, why do we feel so ordinary? Why do we not feel enlightened, free, powerful, fearless, and wise? Why do we not show up like Mother Teresa, Gandhi, and Martin Luther King (or whomever else you may admire)? Herein lies the primordial paradox of wisdom-nature. Everyone is a sage at heart, but everyone is also a sage to be. Everyone is a diamond, but a diamond in the rough. That is the meaning of potential. The spiritual sage lives within us from square one, but we do not fully embody her until the last mile of the journey.

A great meditation master and Indian sage of the fourth century, Asanga, compared this potential to a gold mine. We may know the gold is in there and be aware of its great value. But it does not become useful until we put the effort into mining, unearthing, and refining it. Likewise, we need to compile spiritual tools and use our ingenuity to extract wise qualities from the ground of our being. Until then, potential shows up caked with the earth of suffering, confusion, suspicion, ignorance, anger, fear, anxiety, depression, uncertainty—we could name a hundred spiritual impediments that prevent the full blossoming of love and wisdom. It is up to us to clean up that potential, enjoy the wealth, and share the wealth with others. The whole of the spiritual quest can be seen that way: a process of nurturing innate spiritual genius so that it blossoms into the actions of a spiritual virtuoso.

So, for Day One of your spiritual journey, look into your own experience and inquire whether you have a "most authentic self." What does wisdom feel like? What are its qualities? Think back to times in your life when you felt most at ease, most *real*, most yourself. One of my students identifies with a time when she was a young girl and her parents used to take her camping. As her senses filled with the smell of pine needles, the sound of the breeze in the treetops, and the sight of the dust motes circling in the sun's rays, something changed for her. It was as if everything fell away, and all she had was herself: not her name or her identity, but some kind of self beyond a self.

Memories such as these ground us in an experience of well-being and centeredness connected to our most authentic self. Remembering those times may not be a full-blown experience of wisdom-nature, but it puts us in a space of stability, calm, and authenticity that predisposes us to know wisdom-nature. We might still not have a clear idea about what constitutes our deepest self, but we have a taste or glimpse of that self in moments of well-being, in moments when our experience is more unified and less discursive.

Exercise for Day One

Reflect on Your Wisdom-Nature

In a quiet space, reflect on this question: when have you felt deeply at home in your own skin? To get at this question, think about one time in your life when you have felt most at peace, calm, grounded, or at one with everything. Use memory. Think of one specific time when you felt this way. This time might be a recent one or one in your childhood. Return yourself to that time and relive the feeling of centeredness, oneness, or peace you had then. Consider, does the "deeper self" that you connected with then ever go away? Or is it always present? Does it leave you, or do you leave it?

When you rest in this "deeper self," you may not be able to name it or describe it. You may not even be able to find something that is a self when you try to hold onto it. Even that is not a problem! If you find nothing, rest in the groundlessness of the experience of *not* finding. As a famous Buddhist parable goes, "Not finding is finding." Wisdom-nature is not a thing, so it cannot be identified or pointed to as a thing. It is not even a self, so it cannot be truly found. Even so, everyone has wisdom-nature, and each person senses it at a deep level. No matter what your past, no matter what you may have done, you are divine at heart, and you intuitively know it.

Day Two

Struggle: A Sign You Desire to Awaken

Happiness is different from pleasure. Happiness has something to do with struggling, enduring, and accomplishing.
—George Sheehan

Today's Date: _____

*Y*our wisdom-nature may not be easy to see, but it leaves signs of its presence. Your wisdom-nature, like an animal that moves across a snowfield at night, leaves its traces in your consciousness and body. Initially this seems hard to believe—after all, how many of us feel enlightened? But if wisdom lives in you, it cannot fully escape your notice, even if you do not consider yourself a wise or insightful or intelligent type. One of the great things about contemplation of the wisdom-nature is that anyone is capable of it. One meditation text says, "When it comes to realizing your nature, it does not matter whether you are smart or dumb." Whew—that is a relief.

Dharma Tip

Each day, before reading on, review the previous day. What was your experience of the exercise for Day One? When you look inward to sense your *deepest self* today, does it seem the same as it was yesterday? Did you write anything in the margins? What did you write? Your experiences and insights are the book within the book. These are your everyday dharma.

So what are the signs of your wisdom-nature, and how do you look for them? Fortunately, they are right here, in the field of everyday experience.

Some time back, I was having lunch with a friend and her twelve-year-old daughter. My friend said, "Guess what Kate wants to be when she grows up? She wants to be a schoolteacher." Kate interrupted. "No, I do not, Mom. When I grow up, I want to be *happy*."

Sound familiar? Children begin with a wish that extends throughout a lifetime. Everyone without exception has the wish to be happy and comfortable and to avoid pain. It is only human. How much energy do we put into avoiding what is painful and unpleasant and trying to acquire what is comfortable and pleasant? How many hours a day do you spend working for happiness? To pay the bills for a nice car, for health insurance, for school, for a comfortable home? For most of us, it is almost every waking moment.

But what are we really reaching toward? What is the underlying nature of our struggle? We certainly do yearn for happiness, even if it is sometimes hard for us to define happiness for ourselves. But we are also reaching for a kind of freedom. We wish for freedom to pursue happiness and freedom to be happy. The inevitable flip side to this wish is a desire to be free from the *opposite*—suffering. A teacher of mine once put it this way: "The incessant search for happiness is really a desire to be free in disguise."

We know we long to be free in some obvious ways—free from our mother-in-law's unexpected visits, free from physical pain, free to speak our minds. We all want to be free from something or free to do something. But when you get that particular freedom, whatever it is, do you not find something else that bothers you? When the headache is gone, do we not notice the backache? When the backache is gone, do we not notice that we are irritated at something or someone? We long for freedom, but our small freedoms do not last long! Our natural human angst—restlessness, agitation, discontent, or whatever we label it—kicks in to move us on to looking for the next freedom or the next vista of imagined happiness.

The reason we are not content for long with whatever freedoms we acquire is that the freedom we really seek is bigger: it is too big to be satisfied with merely getting over a headache or a backache. As soon as we get over those, the real ache, our deepest ache, sets in: we are really aching to be free *in the biggest possible way*. That is why we cannot be satisfied for long with any given small freedom. That is what my teacher meant when he said, "The incessant search for happiness is really a desire to be free in disguise." We do not want to be free from suffering for an hour, or a day, or a year. If we had our way, we would be free from suffering—all our neuroses, struggles, and problems—for good. Or at least we would learn to live with them more harmoniously. The same goes for our less-acute pains, like boredom, numbness, and feelings of disconnection or alienation. We would rather be awake, conscious, and wise. We would rather be that way because, at some level, we know we are meant to be.

That is why we struggle. Struggle, the urge to escape and be free, the restlessness that pushes you from one experience to the next, is your wisdom-nature speaking. The existential angst that you generally seek to avoid is the displaced call of your soul wishing to awaken. Asanga put it this way:

> If the wisdom-nature were not present,
> There would be no longing to transcend suffering,
> Nor striving and devotion toward this aim.

If your wisdom-nature—the authentic aspect of yourself that wants to awaken—were not a part of you, you would not be interested in reaching and striving, and there would be no fuel for your spiritual journey. Angst, therefore, is not a bad thing. It is the wisdom-nature in you that reaches for goals. It is the wisdom-nature in you that strives to find peace. It is the wisdom-nature in you that motivates your search for happiness and fulfillment. It is the wisdom-nature in you that is dissatisfied with mediocrity. It is the wisdom-nature that calls for wholeness. The challenge of the seeker is to recognize the potential of that tremendous drive for freedom and channel it constructively. The spiritual journey is about not eliminating angst but learning to make it work for you.

Exercise for Day Two

Analyzing Struggle

Find a place and time when you can quiet your mind and body for a few minutes. Consider an issue you are struggling with. Instead of focusing on the details of the struggle—the objects and people involved—focus on the feeling around the issue. Simply rest in the feeling. As you breathe out, imagine the feelings of stress and struggle being released and going out of your body with the breath.

Now, in a calm state, reflect on the recent feeling of stress. Ask yourself: *When I was struggling, when I was discontent, what was the cause of my struggle? Was it caused by outer conditions? My mind? My body?* Take some time to examine your experience for the ultimate source of struggle.

Day Three

Caring:
A Sign of Compassion

My heart has become a bird which searches in the sky. Every part of me goes in different directions. Is it really so that the one I love is everywhere?

—Rumi

Today's Date: _____

The University of Chicago's National Opinion Research Center recently launched a national altruism study that found most Americans hold altruistic values and perform altruistic actions fairly often. The University of Chicago researchers examined three areas of human thought and behavior related to altruism: altruistic values, altruistic behaviors, and empathy. It found that all three are common in American society. This is just one of an increasing number of scientific studies on the topics of empathy and altruism indicating that we are not just socialized to care about others of our species—we are wired for it.

Even if you are not confident of your potential for empathy, or feel that empathy is what you do in your better moments (but not at other times), you can be certain that you *care* about someone or something every day. Caring is an even more basic affective state than empathy. While empathy involves identifying with another person's situation or suffering, caring is a form of sustained attention to something, mixed with some degree of liking or attachment.

Who and what do you care about most in life? To identify what you care about, look into where you spend your time and energy. Over the next twenty-four hours, take a few moments—now and then—to ask yourself a simple question: *on what are my thoughts dwelling now?* When going about your daily life—washing dishes, waiting in line, and so forth—occasionally observe the direction of your thoughts and drives. This will give you a window into what you care about. Try not to judge or manipulate your thoughts. Just observe. For this exercise to work, observing is sufficient. Observing alone is enough to be transformative. Most of our thinking is so habitual that we are not always even fully conscious of the content of our thoughts. The point is to become more mindful of your impulse to care and to notice where your caring energy is spent. You may be surprised at what you see. Jot down a few things that come to mind when you think, *who and what do I care about?* Just observing where your thoughts are drawn is the first step to getting acquainted with the raw energy of your natural impulse to care. You will need this awareness on your spiritual journey—it is the basis for developing good intention, love, and compassion.

I recently read a memoir of a drug addict who said about the time he was addicted, "I didn't care about anyone or anything. I just wanted to get high and destroy myself." My thought was that, to the contrary, he cared very much. At the time of his addiction, he cared about getting high and destroying himself. That is a kind of caring. There is an energy, a drive, a devotion that comes even with the most destructive forms of caring. If you can recognize the energy of caring in yourself—regardless of the object—you can learn to harness the energy of the caring itself and turn that energy into compassion.

Exercise for Day Three

Observing Your Thoughts and Drives

Three or four times today, ask yourself the question: *What am I caring about at this moment? Where is my energy going?* Try to catch yourself before you have time to manipulate your thinking. By observing your thoughts in this way, you begin to notice where your caring energy is actually going. Once you have done that, consider: *What do I really want to care about? Where do I want to send this energy?* Use the space below to list three things/people/areas/goals/dreams you want to care about, three areas where you want to channel your energy as part of your spiritual journey:

1. _____

2. _____

3. _____

Day Four

Being Aware: A Sign of Wisdom

The body? Drop it as if it were a corpse. Leave it as if it had no owner. The mind? Let it be, as if it were the sky.

—Machig Labdrön

Today's Date: _____

As you read these words, you are aware of their shape, their color, their placement on the page, and their meaning, all at the same time. In Tibetan, the word for awareness is *rigpa*. Awareness is so close to us that we hardly notice it much of the time. We take awareness for granted, like our nose, our eyesight, or our spouse (just testing to see if you were paying attention!). Attention is a good clue that we have awareness. When you are paying attention to something, or when you are surprised into paying attention, your awareness is a little brighter and more obvious. The act of paying attention draws you back into the moment of present awareness, away from your story lines and thinking about the past or future.

Meditations that bring you into contact with momentary awareness gradually move you in the direction of innate wisdom. In the Buddhist tradition, the more you develop an ability to simply *be*, the closer you come to wisdom. Why? Because your wisdom-nature is self-revealing. Simply being aware in the moment, without any effort or any acting out, is a profound method for allowing your innate wisdom to emerge on its own. When you are simply and nakedly aware, it is possible to enter a state of being in which you cease to follow your internal dialogues, your projections, and your plans. You give yourself up to the moment. In the long term, a space opens up for you to know your innate wisdom profoundly and directly.

The word *wisdom* sounds so far away in time, like something that we will achieve later, after getting a head of gray hair, after years of life experience and effort. But it is really as close as your own mind. The Buddhist tradition identifies two kinds of wisdom: analytical wisdom and innate wisdom. While analytical wisdom is trained and developed, innate wisdom is always with you and can only be allowed to emerge. In Tibetan, one word for innate wisdom is *yeshe*, which means "primordial wisdom" or "always having known." Primordial wisdom is a kind of knowing you have had since the day you were born. This wisdom is not something newly created in the mind or acquired from somewhere outside yourself. It is your wisdom-nature.

One of the most direct ways that Buddhists train to discover innate wisdom is through meditation. Meditation should follow us from the very beginning of a spiritual journey to the very end. One simple wisdom meditation is called the Three Arrivals. This is a very basic practice for discovering how to be simply aware; or, to put it in other terms, *how to be simply present here and now*. When we are simply present in the here and now, wisdom emerges naturally.

Most of the time, we are not *here now*. We might be literally someplace, like on a bench in Central Park, or in our living room, or in a garden. You might literally inhabit some time, like 3:00 p.m. on a Thursday or 10:00 a.m. Sunday morning. But chances are your mind is somewhere else. You are thinking about that vacation you are planning next summer, or the conversation you had this morning, or the book you are reading. The meditation of the Three Arrivals is about returning to an awareness of the moment, arriving in the here and now. This can be done anywhere, anytime.

First, simply arrive with your body. Exhale your physical tension audibly. *Ahhh.* Stretch out. Relax. Let go. Shift into minivacation mode. The Three Arrivals is indeed the best five-minute vacation you can have. Just sit perfectly at ease. Let your body be natural. Let go of tension in your shoulders and muscles. Give your body permission to give up doing things. Loosen up, unwind, and chill, as they say.

Now arrive with your breath. Let it be natural. Instead of breathing the breath, let the breath breathe you. Have you ever seen a baby sleeping and the calm and rhythmic way it breathes? This is how the breath settles out when you let it come and go naturally. When you breathe, simply be present with the breath. Let it feel effortless.

Now arrive in the here and now with the mind. Let go of thoughts about the past. Stop planning and anticipating the future. Give yourself permission to just be. Other than being simply aware, there is nothing at all to do! If you do nothing, the mind arrives. Just showing up in the moment is enough. This is your most natural self. Be a nonachiever. Be simple. *Simply be.*

When you are resting like that, thoughts will not stop. That is okay. Thoughts are not a problem in themselves. Thoughts are like fish-bait. If you stop biting at the bait, you will not get hooked. If you leave thoughts alone, they will not harm you. Instead of following your usual tendency to get involved with thoughts, be content with just being aware of them as they come and go. If they become distracting, as soon as you notice your mind has wandered from the present moment, remember that you have all day to be involved with your thoughts. This is your five minutes of taking a break from downloading their junk e-mail.

Keep your meditation session short. If you really like it, you can repeat the meditation later in the day. Remember: five quality minutes is better than ten distracted minutes.

The meditation of the Three Arrivals is the foundation of meditation practice and is used as a preparation for all the contemplation and meditation practices in this book. If building a meditation practice were like making a sandwich, the Three Arrivals would be the first piece of bread. So if you have time this week, do it every day, until next week's meditation practice is introduced.

Meditation is like learning to drive. At first you might feel hyperalert or awkward doing it, but after awhile it feels as if the car drives itself.

From day one, meditation will recharge your batteries. Eventually, it will introduce you to the landscape of your innate wisdom.

Exercise for Day Four

Meditation on the Three Arrivals

First, arrive with your body. Settle your body in a comfortable position. Exhale audibly: *Ahhh.* Feel your muscles relax. Let your body feel at ease and natural.

Second, arrive with your breath. This means to let the breath breathe you. Let your breath be easy and natural. It also means to be at ease with silence. Take refuge in silence for a few moments.

Third, arrive with the mind. Do not think about the past or anticipate the future. Settle into this present moment with effortless ease. Take a break from "doing" and simply be aware. Rest in naturalness and simplicity.

Day Five

The Body:
A Sign of Natural Power

I've seen no place of pilgrimage more blissful than the body.

—Saraha

Today's Date: _____

The body is everyone's most overlooked resource. Simply by virtue of being alive, you have a natural power to act, to learn, to develop, to give, to awaken, and to influence and benefit others. The body is not only useful on your spiritual quest—it is essential. Shantideva, a great sage who lived in eighth-century India, said:

> Think of this body as a boat, and then make as much effort as possible
> to cross the ocean of samsara.

Samsara refers to the cyclic wheel of self-perpetuating craving, anger, and ignorance that causes us to experience suffering in life. To "cross the ocean of samsara" therefore means to shake free of our habitual ways of perpetuating confusion and suffering. Your body—meaning the whole organism that is you—is like a boat, because it is the vessel carrying you throughout your spiritual odyssey to awakening. Where else is the process of waking up going to happen other than within you? While you can arrange some conditions conducive to awakening your wisdom-nature, you already have the basis that you need for that awakening right now: your body.

But having a body is not only significant to spiritual development. The body is also your instrument to change the world. This change is

31

not something that will happen sometime in the future, when you are *really* a sage. You already change the world by virtue of being in it, every single day. The Buddha taught a *law of interpenetration*: that everything interpenetrates everything else. Everything is dependent on everything else. Everything is connected, so that if something happens somewhere in the world, everything else is affected. We now know this to be true on a subatomic level, but the Buddha applied this law mainly to the thoughts and actions of living beings. These days, with the world getting smaller and communication getting quicker, we can more easily notice how intimately our thoughts and actions interpenetrate the thoughts and actions of others. What you think and do inevitably affects others. Therefore, just by virtue of your presence in this world, by virtue of your body's membership in a family, a society, and the human race, you have a biological and social impact on the entire world every day.

By having a body you also act as a model. Just by virtue of being around other people, you—including your actions, attitudes, and speech—will inevitably be noticed. Chances are, people will, either consciously or unconsciously, model themselves after you or sometimes in contrast to you. In a study recently conducted at Harvard Medical School, researchers discovered that when a person watches an action taking place, a number of their brain cells act in the same way as if that person him- or herself were engaging in the action. So if you watch someone eating an ice cream cone, your brain behaves as if you were eating it.

The researchers have named these brain cells *mirror neurons*, because they automatically mirror what they see. The researchers conducting the study postulated that these neurons might explain to some degree why we empathize, why we cry at the movies, and why we emulate certain behaviors after seeing them. This research is interesting in light of the power we have in being alive. You cannot avoid being a participant. Therefore you already do one of the things that sages do best: you act as a model. You already are an example. Right now, for better or for worse, you are modeling behaviors and thoughts for others, so you might as well model good ones.

This is both a great responsibility and a great privilege. The process of awakening is to some extent about going from being an unconscious model to a conscious one. It is worth pausing for a moment to consider the power of the human life that you have right now. Mentally enumerate to yourself some of the gifts that your life offers you. Are you really using these gifts as you would like? Are you a good model? Are your actions in harmony with what, deep down, you would consider a meaningful life? Are you trying to live consistently with what you believe inside, or are you conforming to someone else's expectations? These are questions that most of us struggle with now and then, but the small responsibilities of daily living take over and we forget to reevaluate our existence.

Some of these questions can be answered by developing a fresh appreciation for our very being. We tend to wake up every day taking our body for granted. We take our life, our consciousness, and everything around us for granted, too. How often do we stop to really think about the fact that our presence here is not at all guaranteed from day to day? This was once brought home to me succinctly by a wonderful meditation master named Khenpo Tsultrim. Khenpo Tsultrim is not like the many Buddhist teachers who are willing to talk to their students about all kinds of things, from the weather to relationship problems. Khenpo has not styled himself a therapist-lama. Or a buddy-buddy guru. Or a relationship consultant-slash-spiritual teacher. He does not do much in the way of small talk. Instead, he is known for his tendency to overlook all things routine and to speak the truth—sometimes the uncomfortable truth, or the far-out, ultimate truth. Some students have found themselves taken aback by his directness, but most people are charmed (if not slightly puzzled) by his refusal to descend into mundane communication. Case in point:

I once had the honor of hosting him at a rural retreat center in Virginia. I brought him tea every morning after he woke up. One morning, he walked out of his room, stretched his arms in the air, and declared, "Amazing!"

Week One

"What is it?" I asked, looking around. I thought perhaps he meant the sunrise. Or maybe a coyote had wandered below the window. Or maybe something unusual had surprised him this morning.

Rinpoche's eyes grew wide. "Amazing that I did not die last night!"

Is it not amazing that any of us actually wake up on any given morning? Given the fragility of life, it is a miracle that we avoid death day by day. I will never forget the sense of delight that Khenpo Rinpoche expressed that morning stemming from something as simple as waking up to the surprise, the miracle, the gift of being alive. No single day on this earth need be taken for granted. Life is a windfall, not a profit; a gift, not a given. And it is one powerful gift. If your wisdom-nature had no body to inhabit—if it did not have real, physical contact with a family, a community, and the world—it would have no power to move into action. It would have no power to manifest any of its potential for compassion and wisdom. It would have no power to benefit others. Your physical body is the temple of your wisdom-nature . . . its church and its channel. That is the reason the body is one of the greatest resources you have.

But we are only in this boat for a relatively short time. Some Tibetan texts compare life to a flash of lightning: very powerful and very brief. It is easy for us to think, *Yeah, I know*. You may have considered this before, but do you really *live your life as if you knew*? In 2005, my father began having headaches and a persistent backache. For some time, the doctors prescribed painkillers. When the symptoms persisted, the doctors examined him further. They eventually found metastasized lung cancer. He called me after the diagnosis. "How do you feel?" I asked. "I am dealing with it so far," he replied. "But one thing gets me." There was a pause on the line, and I could hear my father thinking about how to put it into words. "I thought I was immortal."

He was not heavy when he said it. There was a tone of humorous irony, and despite our sadness, we could not hold back a shared chuckle. It was a bittersweet moment. We laughed because it was such a cliché, but it hit home so deeply at that moment. Do we not all think we are immortal? Do we not all expect to wake up tomorrow and many tomorrows after that? In reality, you are a temporary resident of this boat, so do not put off your spiritual journey until your boat starts to sink! This body's simple presence in the world, as brief as our stay is here, is the most overlooked power behind wisdom. Having your life is like having a jewel in the palm of your hands. How will you make use of it?

Even if you see yourself as far from perfect, even if you believe you are a negative influence on those around you, even if you feel as though you have made grave mistakes in your life, you can still be sure that people sometimes admire things about you, sometimes learn things from watching and listening to you, and sometimes even look up to you. You already have a certain kind of natural power, by virtue of living in a family, a community, and a society. It is a power that you have probably overlooked or undervalued most of your life. The natural power of being a member of the human family gives us a constant opportunity to influence others. When you recognize this opportunity, you look for ways to be a good model instead of a mediocre or a bad one.

The body is the crucible for enlightenment. The body itself is the basis for our power and influence in the world. How can a sage be a model for others if he is not present? How can he act with no body to act with? The wisdom-nature is impotent without the body. Therefore, you are already powerful by virtue of simply having a body. You already act as a model for others simply by being in the world with your body and mind—for better or for worse. It is a big responsibility and a big opportunity. How you use it is up to you.

Exercise for Day Five

Reflection on the Gift of the Body

Begin this exercise with the Three Arrivals.

Now take a few minutes to let your mind relax. When you relax the mind, it will look for something to do. Give it something to do by settling your attention on the breath. After a few minutes of focusing on the breath, move your attention into the body as a whole organism. Feel the warmth of your body, your breathing, the feeling of the air on your skin. Practice this meditation of body awareness for a few minutes.

Next, take a moment to contemplate the gift of the body. Consider how this body has carried you through life, supported every experience of joy, and endured every experience of sorrow. Feel gratitude toward your body. Now consider: *How can I be kind to my body? In what ways do I take it for granted?* Think of three ways to repay the kindness of the vessel that holds your life. For example, *I will eat fruit instead of a doughnut for breakfast on weekdays; I will exercise four times a week; I will get another hour of sleep on the weekends.* Whatever ways you think of to be kind to your body, be very specific.

After your meditation is over, write these three ways down.

I will repay my body by:

1. _____

2. _____

3. _____

Day Six

Admiration:
A Sign You Are Gifted

Everything has its wonders, even darkness and silence, and I learn, whatever state I am in, therein to be content.

—Helen Keller

Today's Date: _____

We develop the ability to admire early in life. When I was about ten years old, I went through a phase of fascination with everything to do with Helen Keller. Helen Keller, as you may know, was a pioneer for the rights of the disabled. By her life example, she also permanently reshaped society's expectations of what is possible for the visually and hearing impaired. Helen, born in 1880, was stricken completely blind and deaf in infancy by a bout with scarlet fever. In the late nineteenth century, children like her were considered unreachable and unfit for schooling and were institutionalized as a rule. Helen was—by all expectations—destined for a life of isolation and mental deterioration, punctuated by an early death in an institution for the deaf and blind.

Helen's mother, however, against all expert advice, resisted institutionalizing her daughter and instead hired a tutor, Annie Sullivan. With Sullivan's help, Helen managed—as a child—not only to learn to communicate, but to read Braille, speak, and write. She also learned to read French, German, Latin, and Greek in Braille. She later attended Harvard University and graduated magna cum laude, going on to a successful career as a public speaker, consultant, activist, and writer. In addition to becoming an advocate and activist for people with disabilities, she was also a women's suffragist and pacifist. Evaluation and education of the deaf and blind was never the same again.

I read Helen Keller's autobiography several times and was especially interested in the details of her young life. This may be because I was a kid myself, or because I once had scarlet fever, or because I was afraid of the dark. Her life inspired me, especially the way she took the cynicism of those around her as a challenge. Where other people saw "impossible," she proved anything is possible. When other people doubted her abilities or questioned her potential for success (or the potential success of others like her), she grew more determined and optimistic. She seemed to have an innate courage and fortitude that many people lack, even in the best of circumstances. After the light went out in my bedroom at night, I thought of Helen Keller—who spent a whole life in darkness— and it was easier to relax.

It may be a cliché, but in youth we have a sense of limitless possibility—a sense that we might become like our heroes if we tried. But often that sense weakens as we grow older, as our internal cynic develops, and as the realities of life set in. If you work as a teacher or a counselor or are just a good friend, you will sometimes hear variations on the following statements coming from perfectly good people, even people you think of as the epitome of success: "I do not feel very lovable," or "I am just not a very good person," or "When I weigh the good and bad in myself, the bad ends up winning," or "I cannot shake my fears about the future."

Even the most successful people have some version of this kind of internal monologue sometimes. For some people it is stronger than for others. At the same time, we compare ourselves to others and think, *He is so smart. She is so happy. He is so disciplined. . . . I wish I were like that.* We see in others qualities that we wish we had, but all too often we write ourselves off as essentially incapable of being like them. It is as if we have given up being truly inspired because we do not trust our aptitude for heroism. We think we are not gifted.

But you *are* gifted—it comes with your wisdom-nature. How do you know that? Because you could not recognize a gifted person if you were not gifted yourself. Think of one person you admire. It might be a relative, a friend, or a popular figure. See this person in your mind's eye. Now think of one single quality you admire in that person—no, not nice hair! Something like courage, or kindness, or cheerfulness. Try to put a label on it. It can help to remember some specific times you saw something remarkable shine through this person. What quality did this remarkable "something" have?

I think about the expression on the face of one of my spiritual teachers when he leaned down to hug a student. Someone captured this moment on film. He looked much like my grandmother, who was a kind and gentle woman. It was an expression of complete and total kindness and acceptance. It was the kind of expression a mother has for her only child. I will never forget that moment or the expression on his face. If I were to label the quality that went with that look, I would call it unconditional love.

Try to sum up the best quality of the person you admire in a single word like *kindness,* or *courage,* or *patience,* or *perseverance.* Or try a phrase: *My sister has a "just do it" way about her,* for example. Write that one remarkable quality in the margin of this page.

Now, why do you admire that particular quality in that person? We often think, *I admire that quality because I lack it.* Or we might think, *I admire that quality because I am weak in it.* But the truth is, *you could not admire that quality if you did not already have it yourself.* You could not admire that quality if you yourself were not gifted—even a little—in that regard. It is the latent gifts in you that bridge the gap (of circumstances, time, and space) between you and your heroes.

Even if you live a very different life from a person you admire, as I did from Helen Keller, you identify with that person's challenges and how they overcame them. Your dormant potential recognizes commonality—it sees its own reflection in the heroic qualities that exemplify awakened potential. It is the recognition of commonality that allows you to feel inspired, even if you still feel like you have a long way to go.

The feeling *I have a long way to go* is also a clue that you already have the seed of the destination, that you are the keeper of gifts. You feel as if you have a long way to go because you sense that you start from *somewhere.* You have a long way to go from where you are to where you want to be. This is a start. To put it another way, you could not identify the destination if you did not see the starting point. You could not recognize a hero if you did not have a hero's heart yourself.

Over the years, some people find themselves with a growing list of personal heroes—people they admire and look up to. But other people find themselves with a dwindling list. If your list is dwindling, there is no reason to despair! It is probably not because heroes are becoming less frequent in your life but rather because you are not seeing the heroes around you, or not looking for them. Thinking back to your childhood might be helpful. For many people, childhood is when we first discover heroes—mentors, sages, friends, and even characters in books after whom we model ourselves. In a workshop, I once asked people to write down for me some of their personal heroes. The lists included grade school and high school teachers, fictional characters, parents, pets, friends, spiritual mentors, students, relatives . . . the list was long. In the past, you also admired people like this. You probably had good reasons to do so, and therefore these old heroes from your childhood may still be useful to you.

A personal hero does not have to be alive, and a personal hero does not have to be perfect. A personal hero is someone who teaches (or has taught) you in some way just by being who they are. All you need to identify a personal hero is to think of *one* quality you admire about *one* person. That is enough to start! No single person is likely to fit all the hero criteria you might dream up. But a number of people taken together can make up a hero portfolio that displays many of the qualities that you admire and wish to emulate.

You might admire your aunt for her patience, your father for his toughness, Archbishop Desmond Tutu for his courage. For some of us, one or two people really will stand out as strong mentors or models. That has been true for me with regard to my spiritual teachers. Who are your personal heroes?

Day Six

Exercise for Day Six
Recognizing Your Innate Qualities

Find a quiet place to do this contemplation. First, think of someone you admire. What is one quality you admire in one person? If you could sum up this quality in one word, or phrase, what would it be?

Now, think of a time—recently—when you manifested that quality yourself. If the quality is patience, for example, think of one time you were patient, even just a little. Take a moment to acknowledge the seed of this quality in yourself. Appreciate its presence. Where there is a seed, there is the basis for further development. How can you imagine yourself applying this quality in your life more frequently? In what areas of your life would you do so?

Day Seven

The Power of Emulation

If you meet someone who causes your defects to wane, and your positive qualities to grow like a waxing moon, cherish that sacred friend more than your own body: that is the practice of a bodhisattva.

—Ngulchu Thogme

Today's Date: _____

Patrul Rinpoche—a venerable Tibetan meditation master of the nineteenth century—said, in the context of following a spiritual guide, "Those who emulate well, turn out well." He did not mean that you have to be an impersonator on the road to spiritual success but rather that you can and should learn selectively from the example of the skillful, strong, wise, and compassionate people you meet in life. Learning selectively means developing skill at noticing the strengths of others and taking inspiration from the qualities you admire in them.

This takes a little humility, and you may find excuses not to do so. For example, if your fault-finding mindset weighs in, you might overlook a heroic quality that is worth emulating: *Uncle Jeff has too many faults for me to emulate his (admittedly outstanding) ability to concentrate on the task at hand.* Or you might just feel like you cannot measure up: *I am not good enough or capable enough to try to be like the Dalai Lama.* Or you might think that by emulating someone's thought, speech, or behavior, you are untrue to your sense of self, or you are faking it: *I admire how soft and compassionate my friend Joan is, but it is not me to act that way.*

Try to get around these thoughts by considering, *Who is "me" anyway?* We choose who we want to become from moment to moment.

What we do, we become. Would it be better to stay stuck in the same old rut—comfortable and familiar as it is—in the name of protecting a superficial idea of what *me* is? Do not be afraid to leave your old habits behind long enough to try on new ones. If you admire something about someone, do not let it rest at that. Let the sage in him or her inspire the sage in you! Take a risk to act or think for a moment like this person might. It may fit or it may not, but you cannot know until you try. Since you already unconsciously emulate people around you, why not take the step to make your choices conscious? Emulating consciously or mindfully is a way to transform the inspiring people who surround you into prototypes for wise thought and action.

Emulation does not preclude originality. Emulation empowers it. Originality, creativity, and flexibility are indispensable to unearth and develop our innate potential. Without them, we would lack the necessary fluidity and spontaneity that characterize a spiritual journey. It takes originality and ingenuity to step back from our mental habits and patterns, consciously reflect on their usefulness in life, and then be willing to try new behaviors. Originality is also a quality that allows us to excel in reverse-emulation: the practice of defining the self in opposition to a model or norm.

Before we emulate, we admire. Admiration is a *remedy* for negative mind-states. Why a remedy? Admiration cures you of some harmful states of mind, especially jealousy. When you admire someone's positive qualities in a heartfelt way, there is little room for jealousy, envy, anger, or dislike. Therefore, as you might use a medical remedy to treat illness, you can consciously invoke admiration to remedy the illness of jealousy and dislike in your heart when you notice it there.

Jealousy, in the Buddhist tradition, is classified as one of the five mental poisons, along with ignorance, craving, anger, and conceit. Why? When you are jealous of someone, there is not much room for love, service, and generosity of spirit. Your thoughts are distracted by disliking the fact that someone has something that you lack. In psychological terms, jealousy and love *reciprocally inhibit* one another. They cancel each other out.

Admiration and emulation give you a constructive place to go with the raw mental energy of jealousy. You can turn that energy toward rejoicing in the person's good example and using it to make yourself a better person. Indeed, there is no better way to appreciate that person's presence in the world: as is sometimes said, "Imitation is the sincerest flattery."

Take a moment to identify three people you admire. You might pick someone from history, someone with a public presence whom you do not know, or someone in your life. Make sure at least one of the people is someone you know. This is good practice for becoming aware of the heroes around you. Remember, just because you choose someone as a model does not mean you want to become just like that person. You can admire someone, model yourself after his or her strong qualities, and still remain the unique person you are. You do not have to fuss too much over your list. You do not have to fret over who the best or most important models might be. Picking three people does not mean you have made an exhaustive list. There are many other heroes out there. But by picking only three, you have something on which you can actually focus. Once you have done this exercise with three heroes, you might think of others to try.

Now reflect on the personality traits, qualities, or actions of these three people. What is it that made you write their names down and not the names of a million other people in the world? If it is someone you do not know personally, what is it about him or her that inspires you? What specifically do you admire about this person's words, actions, or ideas? If it is someone you know personally, think about how you feel around him or her. What about this person (or pet—animals work, too!) puts you at ease or motivates you? In what way does this person encourage you to have faith in others and in yourself? What makes you feel good, safe, or content around this person? You may come up with words like *gentle, brave, compassionate, kind, selfless, strong, intelligent*, or those describing any number of other qualities that make this person seem exceptional to you. Let yourself list qualities that come to you naturally, on the basis of how you understand who this person is and his or her impact on you and the world. You may find it easier to write a sentence such as, "I admire Gandhi because he tried to live a life in which his beliefs and actions were in harmony."

After you have made a concise list of this person's characteristics, or written a sentence or two, underline some of the words on the page that remind you of each of his or her strengths. In the case of my sentence about Gandhi, you might underline *beliefs, actions,* and *harmony*. Or you might try to encapsulate those words into a single character trait like *integrity*. Gandhi was a man of integrity in that he strove for consistency between his principles and his actions.

The words you underlined are your *target traits*. Target traits are characteristics you admire and are drawn to. Chances are you are drawn to traits you want to develop in yourself. Take a minute to look at what you have underlined. Are these qualities you would like to emulate? Circle the ones that strike you as qualities you are actually motivated to develop. Do not be nervous about circling! You are not making a commitment . . . you are conducting an experiment in emulation. Even circling one is a start. You might reevaluate these traits as you move forward on your quest, and that is okay.

Over the course of the next week, occasionally look at your target traits. You might want to recopy them onto other pieces of paper. Tape them over your desk or in some place where you will see them now and then. If you like, you can link the target traits with the hero who inspired them. So, for example, your taped-up piece of paper might look something like this: *Integrity like Gandhi's*, or *Kindheartedness like my grandmother's*. That may not be exactly what you wrote originally, but it reminds you of both the general trait and who inspired it. As part of your experiment, today and next week, take a few steps toward emulating these qualities when you see the opportunity in your own life. In what small ways can you put this attitude into action? Imagine you are conducting a spiritual research experiment. Use whatever phrases work for you to test the power of emulation. One of my favorites is, *What would Buddha do?*

Exercise for Day Seven

Identify Target Traits

- Write down the names of three people or beings who have inspired you.
- Next to each name, in a sentence or list, concisely express what it is about this person (or animal) that inspires you.
- Underline some of the words on the page that reveal each hero's strengths. These are your target traits.
- Tape them up where you will see them now and then.

Three personal heroes:	I admire this person because:
1.	
2.	
3.	

Day Seven

Heeding the call of my soul to be free,
may I discover the wisdom within.
May I cherish life as a gift, not a given.
Inspired by the sages all around me,
may I awaken compassion, wisdom, natural power,
and unearth the gifts of my wisdom-nature.

Limitless is the extent of space,
Limitless is the number of living beings,
And limitless are the karma and delusion of beings—
Such are the limits of my aspirations.
                                                    —Samantabhadra

Week Two

Map Your Intention

Step two is to begin to map your spiritual journey with a life-intention that expresses your deepest hopes and dreams.

*Y*our life is an adventure.

How often does it feel that way? For many of us, much of the time, life feels like a struggle to survive. If your survival needs are met, it might feel like a quest for happiness or satisfaction. Sages—and the sage in you—know life is a quest for something much greater and more meaningful.

Day One

Freedom Is Communal

We all live in suspense from day to day; in other words, you are the hero of your own story.

—Mary McCarthy

Today's Date: _____

*E*very day when you wake up, you are writing a new chapter in your life's story. It could not be anyone else's story, right? Well, maybe it is someone else's story, if you are a novelist. But even the novelist is a storymaker writing two stories—one on the page and one in the notebook of space and time. No matter what you may think or believe, what you do today is going to matter, just as a stone thrown in a pond always makes ripples. Ever since you woke up this morning, you have been throwing stones and leaving ripples that matter to others, to yourself, to the world, and to your own spiritual journey.

The Buddha called this ripple effect the law of karma. By the law of karma he meant something like what Newton meant in his third law of motion: every action has an equal and opposite reaction. On the one hand, the Buddha meant this literally: every movement in the universe has consequences. On the other hand, the Buddha was talking about the integrity of human action. That is, what you reap is what you sow. If you really accept that, it means taking responsibility for whatever happens to you.

One of my students once said to me, "I do not control my life. My life controls me." We all feel that way much of the time. It seems as if we have little freedom over what happens to us every day. Things go down. It is a fact of life. Is there anything we can do about this? We may not be able to change every life condition, but we can change how we feel about our participation in every condition. Spiritual life is a journey from feeling victimized by circumstance to feeling empowered to embrace every circumstance.

In Tibetan, the word for a life's story or biography is *namtar*, which means "complete freedom." A biography, in the Buddhist sense, is a life of freedom, not of limited personal freedoms, but of existential liberty. Existential liberty does not mean freedom from circumstance, freedom from the stuff that takes place every day. It means freedom from self-imposed limitations and freedom from the habit patterns—such as anger, craving, jealousy, and ignorance—that bind us to mental suffering. A sage is not someone who is free from life's inconveniences but rather someone who has become free from reacting to those inconveniences in a dysfunctional way.

What would happen if you woke up every day thinking, *How am I going to compose my life today? How am I going to write this day to become a spiritually freer person? A better person? A wiser person?* You may believe this kind of big thinking is beyond you. But—from the perspective of the ripple effect—if you have a commitment to awakening wisdom, if you have even the smallest urge to become a better, wiser, and more compassionate person, you are already a life-writer of your spiritual odyssey. You are already the protagonist of a life of freedom—in which discovering the path, awakening more fully, and becoming free from the sleep of apathy is a priority. Therefore, today when you woke up, you began to write a chapter in your life of freedom. You started the day on a spiritual journey.

What is a spiritual journey, exactly? We might say that it is a journey with conscious purpose to serve your highest ideals. Simple purpose, by itself, is not alien to us. You may not have articulated a purpose for your life, but that has not kept you from living with purpose. Or put another way, you already *serve* something: you serve a set of ideals, values, and goals that—put together—inform the direction of your life. Bob Dylan put it well in his song "Gotta Serve Somebody." From the moment you were born, your energy moved out into the world, and eventually the world pushed back. In that process of negotiation, you found yourself serving somethings and someones, for better or for worse—it is a matter of survival, and sometimes common sense. Reflecting on who and what you serve is a good start to understanding how to reimagine life as a spiritual quest.

In Buddhist sources, *freedom* is a synonym for *enlightenment*. Since a sage's purpose is to live a life of freedom, of existential liberty, you might think that freedom would be the goal of his or her spiritual life. A seeker plans to become free and enlightened, right? Is not freedom the goal? Many people think that freedom is the goal of Buddhist practice, but that is only partially true. *Freedom* is a synonym for *awakening*, but not your personal awakening. Spiritual freedom is not that exclusive. It cannot be harnessed by any form of self-propelled, self-motivated journeying. If it could, we would blithely scale the mountain of enlightenment alone.

But sages take no joy in reaching the top alone. Not only would that be a selfish journey, but it would not be any fun. It would be like summiting the peak of Everest and having no one to share the champagne with. Real freedom is communal. The ancient Indian sage Shantideva, who has had great influence on the thinking of the Dalai Lama, puts it this way in an exhortation to himself: "O mind, make this resolve: *I am bound to others*." Freedom does not mean escaping from all the complications of relationships and the pain of ordinary life. It means liberation from the bonds of egotism, the true cause of our daily sufferings. If we climb alone, then we care about ourselves alone, and there is no food more nourishing to the ego than selfishness. That is why the Buddha described spiritual freedom as rending the bonds of ego through a path of universal love and compassion that includes everyone.

So a sage does serve somebody. Indeed, a sage serves *somebodies*, and not just his or her spouse, family, community, or country. The spiritual quest of a sage is more encompassing than that. It is a mission, an odyssey, to serve each and every member of the human family. A sage's reason for breathing, acting, living, and following a spiritual path is solely to serve all others. Such service becomes a primary source of joy, enthusiasm, and excitement.

Even when it appears that a sage's body is serving only a specific group or person at any one time—a friend, family member, community, or country—the sage's mind extends beyond to think universally, to live in service of the greater family of humanity and even everything that lives. The sage considers, *How do my thoughts and actions affect the world? Not just some of humanity, not just the people that I like, but all of humanity?*

Exercise for Day One

Contemplating Karma

Take a moment to relax in a quiet place. Breathe. Close your eyes.

Now reflect on your actions from the time you woke up until now. What did you do, think, and feel today? Think even about actions you might consider mundane: making coffee in the morning, shopping, eating.

What kind of effects—mental, physical, and emotional—are you able to observe unfolding from what you did? What impact did you have on others? What impact did your actions have on your mind and body?

Use your imagination and deduction to paint a picture of the karmic ripples that moved out or will move out from your actions today. Especially note states of emotion in yourself and others: When did you feel content and why? When did you feel unhappy and why? Can you find the original "stone" that spread out as the "ripples" of emotion?

Day Two

Chart Your Course with a Life-Intention

Do I contradict myself? Very well, then, I contradict myself. I am large. I contain multitudes.

—Walt Whitman

Today's Date: _____

*A*ctions begin with intention. The life you are living now is formed by intentions. Even before you do something simple, like picking up this book to read it, you first must have decided in your mind, *I will pick up this book*. Likewise, if you want to make any kind of positive change in your life, you have to start making an intention—a decision, a resolution, a plan. You have to decide, *I want to make a positive change in my life, and here is how I am going to do it*.

Therefore, one of the most important aspects of a spiritual journey is *intention*. At the beginning of a physical journey, you need a map. The same goes for the beginning of a spiritual journey: you need a life-map, a plan, a statement of where you are headed and why. A spiritual intention is such a statement. It expresses your purpose for living and acts as a mission statement for life.

Have you ever had an experience that suddenly and unexpectedly put your life into vivid focus? A death in the family, illness, a divorce, falling in love . . . times of intense feeling—pain or joy—when mundane aspects of life lose meaning, when we feel shaken to the core. These are often catalysts for developing a strong sense of life-purpose or intention. Sometimes we simply intend, for the first time, to find answers to the deeper questions: Why do things like this happen to people? What am I doing here? How can I resolve this with the way I have been living my life? How can I live a better life?

If we resolve to live a life serving humanity, our intention cannot be merely self-inclusive. It must include others. It must be relational; it must be a *loving* intention. One of my favorite expressions of loving intention comes from the great Tibetan Buddhist master Yeshe Tsogyal, who lived in seventh-century Tibet. She came home from a journey to discover that one of her gurus had passed away during her absence. She approached the reliquary (*stupa*) that held his cremated remains and offered handfuls of gold dust and silk at the base of the stupa. She wept and sang a prayer of intention, a last tribute to her beloved teacher, vowing to follow his example:

> Perfecting, completing, the activity of the bodhisattva,
> May I become a sharer of teachings and a mentor of teachers;
> Planting the banner of enlightenment forever,
> Crossing the ocean [of existence] in the boat of a human body,
> May I be a mother of beings, their guide and spiritual friend.

Later, Yeshe Tsogyal became an eminent spiritual teacher and scholar whose impact on the Buddhist tradition continues to this day. Yeshe Tsogyal's prayer—drawn out of her by the sorrow of losing her own mentor—is the aspiration of a brilliant teacher. Just as her mentor guided her with a compassionate hand to spiritual transformation, she intends to guide her students, as their spiritual friend, on the path of awakening.

Yeshe Tsogyal's prayer embodies the very essence of a loving life-intention: the intention to awaken in order to be of benefit to, and ultimately catalyze the awakening of, every living being. Her intention was not a plan to attain freedom alone, not a plan to awaken alone . . . but a plan to awaken together with others. It is a statement of purpose that puts everyone in the picture, even if most others do not know they are being included.

I remember the time when I was in college that a graduate student in Buddhist studies gave me a ride in her old VW and first described to me the universality of a sage's (or bodhisattva's) loving intention. I was a little intimidated as well as intrigued. *That objective is admirable*, I thought. *But how could a person—hypothetically—make a prayer that big? Let us say it were me. How could I actually voice such an intention? What if I were to fail in carrying out the intention? What if I fell short?*

After years of wondering about this, I finally came to understand—the more I studied and practiced Buddhism—that the loving spirit behind such a universal intention, and the selflessness needed simply to voice such an intention, is the real juice within the intention itself—not its specific content or whatever future might come of it. It is not about fear; it is about love. Therefore, *we cannot be afraid to intend.*

It is fear that has kept us from accomplishing many of our dreams and goals. How many of your own most heartfelt dreams have you left aside because you were afraid of the risks involved or afraid of failure? The sage's vision is bigger than only this life; it is bigger than a single, limited self. By making an intention, you develop patterns of thought that influence your overall attitudes and behavior. By making the intention to awaken for universal good, you have already succeeded in fulfilling it to some degree. To make such an intention takes courage, commitment, and altruism. These qualities flower over time and translate into awakening the wisdom-nature and into real actions.

Back to Dylan's timely song. To clarify what your life's intention—your personal mission statement—looks like, begin by thinking about what you serve. Everyone places his or her energy into certain goals and hopes. What do you *really* serve in life? What kind of ideals do you hold that inform your actions? Take some time to make an honest assessment. It is one thing to believe you serve an ideal and another thing to act upon that ideal. To what do you really devote the energy of your actions?

Now, what do you *want* to serve? The first step to discovering what your spiritual journey is about is to make an honest and heartfelt intention. An intention is an expression of the desire to serve something. A spiritual intention expresses the desire to serve your highest ideal. It is powerful: it is a promise to yourself to stick to your spiritual journey.

It is always a pleasant revelation and relief to seekers in Buddhist circles when they discover that the Buddha loved options. The more centuries passed between the life of the Buddha and the present day, the more options evolved. By the time Buddhism made its way to Tibet, there was a veritable smorgasbord of ways to live as a seeker and get away with it. That is, by the way, one reason Tibetan Buddhism—one of the most diverse repositories of spiritual lifestyles in Asia—appeals to me.

One sutra describes three kinds of life-intention. I find this classification useful for showing us that there is not just one kind of sage or seeker and that not every path is alike.

Dharma Tip

A *sutra* is a kind of holy text in the Buddhist tradition. The tradition holds that the Buddha himself composed the sutras, but Western scholars believe they were written and edited over the course of many centuries.

The first type of life-intention is called the *king-like intention*. The seeker with this kind of spiritual intention follows the spiritual path like a leader or an individualist. She sees herself as a pioneer, focusing on self-improvement for the sake of the betterment of humankind. Her driving force is ambition, and she sees herself as responsible for others. Like a king, this kind of person develops wisdom and then—on the basis of attaining that powerful place—takes steps to help others.

The second intention is called the *boatman-like intention*. The seeker with this kind of spiritual intention follows the spiritual path in the role of a guide. He imagines spiritual life as a communal endeavor. His slogan for enlightenment is "All or none." Although he is a team leader, he wants to attain the fruits of the path only if his buddies do also. His driving force is the cooperative spirit. Everyone is in the same boat, so to speak.

The third intention is the *shepherd-like intention*. Like a shepherd, this kind of seeker is not very self-involved. As a shepherd's eyes are rarely drawn from her sheep, a seeker with a shepherd's intention cannot take her mind's eye off others. Only after their needs are met does she look after her own. She lives only for the welfare of others and makes sure that whatever resources she obtains go to others first. This kind of person's driving force is love and empathy.

Sages commit to different styles of awakening, but in all cases their focus is on a huge group, the very biggest group: the family of humanity. A sage with a king-like intention wishes to awaken *first* and then lead the family of humanity to awakening. A sage with a boatman's style wants to attain awakening *together with* the family of humanity. The shepherd-like sage wants to attain awakening *only after* everyone else has awakened.

Dharma Tip

Consider: What is your "biggest group"? Is "humankind" too broad, or too limited? What works for you? Some alternatives: "my community," "my family," "livingkind" (human or otherwise)—what form does your spiritual family take?

It just goes to show that a sage might find himself or herself comfortable with one style of intention more than another. You might have confidence in one approach to awakening more than another. You might have an independent spirit and so might make the prayer, "May I awaken so that I may lead others (humanity, my country, my community) to awakening." Or if you are a community-oriented person, you might aspire, "May we all awaken together." Or you might put others first in your mind, and pray, "May I, through my example and my good deeds, inspire others to awaken *first*, and then may I awaken after each and every one of them has made it before me."

The reality, however, is rarely that simple. Most of us will relate to every one of these styles at different points, and we may even develop our own. Our awakening intention will not always take a consistent form. As aspiring sages, we should be sincere, not consistent. Humans are multidimensional creatures, and therefore their intentions will not always look the same from one day to the next—and that is okay, because variety is the spice of life-intention.

Exercise for Day Two

What Do You Serve?

Take a quiet few moments to consider: What do you serve in life? What are a few things/people/causes/organizations/tendencies that you put time and energy into every day (in both the positive and the negative sense)?

In my daily life, I find myself serving (for example, my job, my children, my dogs, my addictions):

1. _____

2. _____

3. _____

Now consider, what more do you want to serve in life? What is your ideal of service?

As I move forward in my spiritual journey, I want to serve (for example, my community, my family, humanity, the earth):

1. _____

2. _____

3. _____

Day Three

Create a Life-Intention

A man is what he thinks about all day long.

—Ralph Waldo Emerson

Today's Date: _____

This week, you will compose a life-intention and aspirations and then compile them in an Awakening Prayer. Today, to start this process, write down an intention that expresses what your life's mission is really about. This is a concise expression of what you, in your heart of hearts, really want to serve. What do you really want to awaken to in this life? Express it in your own words. It should be an intention that you feel comfortable making and that comes from your heart. It should reflect what you value and believe.

While composing a spiritual intention, you don't have to be original. You just have to be sincere. In the Buddhist context, such statements of intention come under the heading of a "vow" because it expresses a personal commitment to a life-purpose. Buddhists often memorize the intentions of sages of the past, or their own spiritual guides, and adopt them as their own. When I lived in a Buddhist monastery, I memorized many intentions of past masters—the Buddha, as well as my other teachers. I often remember these memorized verses, and they remind me of the intention of my own spiritual journey.

I am also inspired by the intentions expressed by my friends and students. At a meditation retreat I led recently, I asked the participants to write down their spiritual intentions. Here is a partial list:

May I awaken in this lifetime.

My spiritual journey is about valuing others. I want to bring joy into the world.

My mission is to be a servant to humanity.

My goal in life is to relieve the suffering of others.

May I shine the lamp of knowledge and plant the excitement of discovery in the minds of children.

My deepest wish is to become fully enlightened, so all beings can be fully enlightened and free from suffering.

May I serve God and God's purpose.

I pray to awaken to the loveliness of my family. I put family first.

My life's purpose is to nurture my children and allow them to become exactly who they are meant to be.

May each and every person awaken, and may I awaken after them. I want to be there to see their awakening.

These are all wonderful examples of mission statements for life, a snapshot into the spiritual lives of people like you starting out on a spiritual path. Below are some intentions expressed by some sages of the Buddhist tradition, ancient and modern. You will notice that intentions are often expressed in the form of prayer. What distinguishes intentions from most prayers is the inclusiveness of their scope. Intentions focus on the big picture and how the seeker sees his or her part in a larger vision.

I, from this time forward until I arrive at the heart of enlightenment, engender great, completely perfect unsurpassable intention to awaken [love and wisdom]. I will strive to guide those who have not crossed over, liberate those who have not been liberated, and shelter those who are oppressed.—*The Buddha; traditional Buddhist prayer*

May we all be free of suffering, obtain sublime happiness, and attain awakening together.—*Kalu Rinpoche, twentieth-century meditation master of the nonsectarian movement of Tibetan Buddhism*

As long as there are living beings in existence, by effortless, spontaneous, beneficent activity, may I ripen and lead them without exception to complete liberation.—*Niguma, eleventh-century female cofounder of the Shangpa lineage of Tibetan Buddhism*

May all beings everywhere with whom we are inseparably connected be fulfilled, awakened, and free. May there be peace in this world and throughout the entire universe, and may we all together complete the spiritual journey.—*Lama Surya Das, twentieth-century nonsectarian American Buddhist teacher*

Buddhists are certainly not the only ones with spiritual or humanitarian intentions on a cosmic scale. Many historical exemplars express their vision of a purposeful life as a quest to serve humanity. Gandhi:

Man becomes great exactly in the degree in which he works for the welfare of his fellow men.

Margaret Mead put it this way:

I personally measure success in terms of the contributions an individual makes to her or his fellow human beings.

B. R. Ambedkar, the leader of the movement for human rights for the untouchables class in India, expressed service as the mark of greatness:

A great man is different from an eminent one in that he is ready to be the servant of society.

Martin Luther King, Jr., expressed his intention in a way that gave voice to the unspoken wishes of thousands, inspiring others to make similar intentions. His dedication to love and selfless service is apparent when he expressed how he hoped to be remembered:

I'd like somebody to mention that day [when I die] . . . that Martin Luther King, Jr., tried to give his life serving others . . . to clothe those who were naked . . . to visit those who were in prison. I want you to say that I tried to love and serve humanity.

King's intention is a celebrated example of how a personal mission can be expressed as a broader quest that rests on the ideals of love and service to humanity, excluding no one.

Today, see if you can compose an intention that expresses how you would envision your ideal spiritual journey. As you compose your life-intention, consider the implications. Given your intention, what would you do to fulfill it? That is not a simple thing. Whether your goal is to serve humanity, or all living creatures, or your family or your community or your country, your commitment to others requires the development of wisdom, compassion, patience, diligence, and selflessness, right down to simple things like taking care of your physical health. In the following chapters, we will focus more on how to translate intentions into action.

Exercise for Day Three

Composing a Life-Intention

Reflect on the purpose of your spiritual journey. What form does serving humanity take for you? To help with this, review the exercises for Day One and Day Two.

It is important that your life-intention make sense to you, given your values and orientation in life. Try to word it so that it is broad enough to encompass your many goals, wishes, and dreams for your spiritual life.

In the space below, compose a life-intention. When composing it, keep in mind that you will certainly edit and revise it. This is just a draft, so do not be afraid to write.

My Life-Intention:

_____

_____

_____

Day Four

Aspirations

Prayer is the spirit speaking truth to Truth.
—James Bailey

Today's Date: _____

In addition to an intention, we can also make aspirations. While an *intention* is a vow or personal commitment setting the tone of your spiritual journey, *aspirations* are specific prayers expressing how that journey might play itself out. Aspirations are your personal wishes in a day-to-day sense; they are the spin-out from the hub of your overall motivation. For example, while your intention may be to serve humanity, your aspiration on a given day might be to refrain from smoking. Aspirations mirror the richness and color of the journey to enlightenment. Since it is a part of the journey to serve a life-intention, taking some time to reflect on the connection between your specific aspirations and your life-intention can be illuminating.

There is a famous story in Tibet about the power of pure aspirations. Tara, a buddha revered throughout Asia, was once a princess named Wisdom Moon (remember that Buddhists think in terms of many lifetimes). In her life as a princess, she developed—for the first time—the intention to awaken fully, to attain enlightenment, for the benefit of others. But the princess put a caveat on her intention. She tacked on a prayer to be reborn again and again, throughout all her lifetimes, as a woman, so that she might inspire women to attain enlightenment. On the basis of that prayer, Tibetans believe, she appears for every generation in the form of a woman—a spiritual heroine.

It is not that the princess thought women were better than men. She looked beyond her personal preferences and asked herself, "What does the world around me need right now?" What the world needed was a female buddha. Somehow, the gender mattered for her time and place, so she aspired to meet the needs of those around her by taking a female form.

Once you are aware of the concept of aspiration, you see it everywhere. Every time someone begins a sentence with "I just wish . . . " or "I would be so happy if . . . " or "I pray that . . . " they are making an aspiration. Not all these aspirations are oriented toward serving others; many, if not most, of the aspirations people (including ourselves!) make are self-serving: *I wish I had enough money to remodel our kitchen. I wish I had a nicer car.* What do we do with these ordinary aspirations that we often make? Should we throw them out?

It is not necessarily skillful merely to jettison such wishes. Instead, you can evaluate them and imagine how they may or may not support your best spiritual intentions. It is possible that remodeling the kitchen has advantages that can support your overall mission to be a good person and to bring happiness to your family. This week, take some time to observe the everyday aspirations that you and others make. Ask yourself, *Is this aspiration reflecting my highest intentions, the ones that I make in my better moments?* If not, consider how you might amend the aspiration to bring it more into alignment with where you really want to go in life. Remember, it is not a promise written in stone but a heartfelt prayer.

It can be helpful when writing your aspirations to reflect on the kinds of aspirations others have made. Here are some aspiration prayers written by my friends and students for themselves:

May I learn to see the good in everyone and not look for faults in others.

May I come to respect and care for my body so that I can be around a long time to serve my family.

May I learn to accept things just as they are.

May I give up smoking.

I pray to become a patient person who is not overwhelmed by her anger.

Here are some aspirations written by friends and students that focus on others:

May my mother, along with all beings, find her way to happiness and fulfillment.

May all those in the world who are suffering find contentment.

I pray that my dog may not suffer long with his illness.

May all those who perform evil actions develop an understanding that they are harming others; may the light of wisdom dawn for them.

Aspiration prayers written by various wisdom masters over the centuries make up a large part of what Buddhists chant every day. Below are some excerpts of the many aspirations that have been made by sages, ancient and modern. I have purposely selected these aspirations to illustrate the wide variety of things that sages wish for.

May I be the medicine and the physician for the sick. May I be their nurse until their illness never reoccurs.—*Shantideva*

May my emotional afflictions arise as a path [to enlightenment].—*Khyungpo Naljor*

If I develop good qualities, may I not be proud. If negative thoughts arise in my mind, may I not consider them defensible.—*Machig Labdrön*

May all those connected to me throughout the three times [past, present, and future]—

Fathers and mothers, their eyes filled with pure love, rulers, their partners,

Ministers and attendants, every level of society, winged creatures, wild beasts,

Every single one—

be completely filled with the ambrosia of awakening.—*The Seventeenth Karmapa*

Week Two

The world we see now is the result of aspirations and prayers—along with all the hopes and wishes—we have made in the past, sometimes unconscious ones. This is evident if you look around at your circumstances. How did you get to the dwelling that you live in? What kinds of wishes, desires, or even mistakes put you here? If you trace back the series of moments that brought you to a certain physical location, you can see the thread of decisions, choices, and coincidences that landed you in this place and not somewhere else on the planet. These decisions, choices, and coincidences were based on aspirations. At some point, you wanted something, and you wished for something. That motivated you to act. Those actions had consequences, and here you are. Therefore, to change this reality in any way, begin with assessing what motivates you. If you do not like what you see, rethink your aspirations.

Your exercise for today is to write down three aspirations. What do you really pray for? What kind of prayers spring to mind when you think about what you really want out of life? What have you prayed for today, this week, this month? Let your inner heart guide your aspirations. Generally, aspirations are more specific than your broad intention, but they may relate to it. Think about how they are related to your intention.

Aspirations are sometimes made for others, or for a community, or for the world. Sometimes they are personal, for your own development or welfare. Nothing is too small to pray for. Very small things can be very significant. If you know that something will better the world, even in a small way, it is worth praying for. If something will make you a better person and move you more effectively onto your spiritual path, it is worth praying for. Sometimes the smallest aspirations lead to the biggest results.

You do not have to limit yourself to three aspirations, but this is a start. Beginning with a few specific aspirations will give you room to observe how these prayers are influencing your life this week. If you make too many prayers initially, you risk overwhelming yourself (if many prayers just come to you, write them down now to add later). As you get used to aspiring, you can add to your Awakening Prayer as you like. There is no limit! You can even include some of the aspirations you read here and others you come across in your life.

Now that you have written these three aspirations, see if you can widen their scope. Compose each aspiration again, experimenting with making it bigger. So, for example, if you aspire, *May my grandmother be relieved from the suffering she is experiencing with cancer*, try widening the scope of your prayer like this: *May all people who have cancer be relieved from their suffering, including my grandmother*. If you aspire, *May I become more patient*, then try, *May I and everyone in my family/community/country/the world become more patient*. Change the prayer, *May I earn enough money to support my family and buy a house*, into, *May all families, including mine, be supported and find shelter*. See how it feels to include more and more people in your prayers. If it feels right to you, you can extend your prayers to animals, even insects.

See how far you can go—extending the prayer to include more and more living beings—and still make the prayer from the heart. If your prayer begins to feel too abstract, stop extending it. When something becomes abstract, it feels like you are just praying in theory. Theory will not transform you.

Prayers must be heartfelt, or sincere, to transform you. Why? If you pray in a way that you think is "right" but you are not moved by your prayer, you will just end up mouthing words. Those words might sound meaningful to someone else, but they will not change you. That is why you must pray for what you really wish for, for what truly moves you. Then your prayer will be heartfelt. Sincere prayers can take limitless forms, as many as there are individuals: *May I have the strength to quit drinking (take care of my body so that I can fulfill my intention)* or *I pray for the gift of a kind heart*. Or *May my daughter get better*. Or *May there be world peace*.

Exercise for Day Four

Composing Aspirations

Compose three aspirations. They might begin with *May . . .* or *I pray . . .* or *I aspire to . . .*

My aspirations:

1. _____

2. _____

3. _____

   Now, how can you expand the scope of these aspirations? How can you make them bigger, more inclusive?

My expanded aspirations:

1. _____

2. _____

3. _____

Day Five

The Awakening Prayer

It is for the purpose of aiding all beings that you set forth on the road of enlightenment.

—The Buddha

Today's Date: _____

The Indian saint Atisha said, "After developing the aspiration to awaken, make a great effort to deepen it." One of the best ways to deepen your intention and aspirations is through prayer. An Awakening Prayer is a combination of your life-intention and aspirations, worded as a prayer. It is called an Awakening Prayer (*bodhicitta* prayer) because it is intended to wake you up to your spiritual motivations and aspirations. You will read, recite, or chant (as your prefer) this prayer at the outset of your spiritual practices and meditations throughout the rest of the book and maybe even beyond the end of the seven-week course.

That is not to say this prayer cannot be edited and might not change from week to week. Remember the spiritual experiment and keep it light. The point is to have an Awakening Prayer practice in place despite the evolving nature of its contents. The purpose of such a practice is to remind you of your overall spiritual intent and goals at the outset of every meditation and contemplation session.

Exercise for Day Five

Compose an Awakening Prayer

Use the space on the opposite page to compose your Awakening Prayer. Simply go back to review the exercises for Day Three ("Composing a Life-Intention") and Day Four ("Composing Aspirations") and copy over what you have written onto your prayer sheet. You might revise it as you go. When you are finished with that, you can call it a day. You have composed your Awakening Prayer!

My Awakening Prayer

Day Six

Deep Prayer

In prayer it is better to have a heart without words than words without a heart.

—Gandhi

Today's Date: _____

*I*nitially, prayer involves giving expression to your deepest wishes. Then it involves sitting with them in quiet and relaxed reflection. Through quiet reflection, a prayer becomes real: it moves from the mouth to the heart.

Prayer is the next layer of the meditation sandwich you started making last week. If the Three Arrivals is the first slice of bread, your Awakening Prayer is the mayonnaise, or whatever appetizing spread you use on your sandwiches. After the Three Arrivals, the next step to constructing a meditation session is to take some time for prayer. Your Awakening Prayer is all you need, although you can expand and develop prayer within your practice as time goes on.

As you did last week, begin by taking some time to practice the Three Arrivals in a quiet place. As you gradually build your meditation practice and become more familiar with previous steps, you can spend less time on them. So now that you are familiar and comfortable with the practice of the Three Arrivals, you can settle into it in a few minutes. After that, read your life-intention aloud, which is the first line of your Awakening Prayer. Take your time as you recite it. You might want to break it up into phrases or individual words. After you say each phrase or word, take a moment to rest quietly with that part of your prayer. Let it sink in. Let the prayer move from your mouth to your heart. Respect the sacredness of your own prayer, and explore its implications.

Day Six

Let us take a very concise intention as an example: *May I awaken in order to benefit others.* If you break it into phrases, the first would be: *May I awaken.* And the second: *in order to benefit others.* You can contemplate each phrase on its own and then put them together. Or if you break your intention into individual words, you can contemplate each word on its own, as if holding individual little gems in your mind.

Going word by word is what I do when I have more time. When I have less time, I work with phrases. Just the three little words *May I awaken* are packed with meaning! Deep prayer is unlocking with your heart the real meaning of prayer. Here is an example of how my thought process goes when I pray word by word:

> **May:** *I pray, beseech, and wish. "May" expresses the heartfelt longing of my prayer . . . a word beseeching the universe, the enlightened presence of my spiritual mentors, the workings of karma, the laws of interpenetration, the force of human love. "May" fills my prayer with faith and trust. "May" reminds me that I rely on forces outside myself to contribute to this quest and make it possible. Most of all, "may" is a word that allows room for me to learn and grow from all outcomes, not just the ones I envision.*

This is only an example. In general, you should pray to whatever or whomever feels right to you. If you believe in a higher power, call on that power when you pray. *But you do not have to believe in a higher power to pray!* Many Buddhists simply trust in the law of interpenetration when they pray, the idea that everything is connected and interdependent.

I know a particle physicist who practices Buddhist meditation, but instead of praying to the Buddha or to spiritual mentors, he prays to—or puts his trust in—the as-yet undiscovered but theorized unified law of physics that connects all things and people. Do whatever works for you. You can pray to your wisdom-nature, your own potential. No matter what the content, deep prayer is effective: it brings inner peace to your heart and mind. Based on the law of interpenetration, your activity of prayer also has the power to affect the world.

I [the next word]: *This intention can be fulfilled by me alone and in this body alone, not by someone else or somewhere else. This intention will only be fulfilled if I do something about it. May I fully and joyfully take this responsibility and gift in hand. May I recognize the wisdom-nature in "I." May I recognize that ultimately the "I" is empty of ego, that the best "I" is selfless. There is no single "I" in the team of humanity. May I and all humanity recognize this life and body as my temple, as an opportunity, and as a gift, not a given.*

Awaken: *To awaken is the purpose of my spiritual journey. May wisdom and love fully awaken in my mind and heart and the minds and hearts of all others. May I engage in the practices that support awakening—in study, reflection, and meditation. May I open my heart to others and open my mind to truth.*

This is just an example of how you can take three individual words and turn them into a contemplative practice. Because your intention and aspirations are unique, your process of prayer will be, too. When you sit with your intention and your aspirations, let them spontaneously inspire you to weave together a contemplative prayer practice. No two prayer sessions are the same! This week, spend more time contemplating your life-intention. The time you spend contemplating your aspirations can be shorter, depending on what feels appropriate to you.

The key to making deep prayer effective is occasionally to take the time to breathe, center, relax, and focus between every word or phrase. Prayer practice is a minivacation. The more relaxed your body is, the more stable and focused your attention will be. So if you find yourself feeling rushed or bored, take three deep breaths and feel tension release on the exhale. Then return to the process of deep prayer.

When you pray deeply, let go of expectation. Deep prayer is without caveats; that is the meaning of the word *may*. There is a difference between aspiring and simply getting your hopes up. To aspire deeply, let go of expectation and anxiety regarding an outcome. The aspiration in itself is the practice, not the attainment of an imagined result. Aspiration makes a space in which all possibilities are allowed to unfold. Let it be, whatever *it* may turn out to be. Deep prayer brings peace of mind, an appreciation for the deep mystery of karma, and acceptance of all outcomes.

At the end of this process of contemplation, sit for a moment in the afterglow of your intention and aspirations. Feel the peace of prayer enfold you. Allow your inner serenity to come forth. The point is to be there while getting there. That is to say, praying is not all about longing and yearning focused on the future. It is also about accepting things just as they are right now and being at peace with what you have.

Exercise for Day Six

Deep Prayer

- Put your Awakening Prayer in front of you, on a table or surface.
- Practice the Three Arrivals (you may want to review this practice from last week).
- Read your life-intention aloud. Take several minutes to reflect on it word by word or phrase by phrase. Remember to breathe, center, relax, and focus.
- Read your aspirations aloud, sitting with each aspiration for a minute or two.
- Let the prayer move from your mouth to your heart. Feel the prayer . . . let it move you.
- Rest in the afterglow of your Awakening Prayer. Breathe. Enjoy.

Day Seven

The Sage's GPS

The big question is whether you are going to be able to say a hearty yes to your adventure.

—Joseph Campbell

Today's Date: _____

When you are on a spiritual journey, it is possible to lose sight of where you are going. The wish to serve humanity, or even any part of it, is a big intention. The fog of everyday concerns can creep in, and you may or may not notice that you have lost track of it. How are you going to know if you are losing sight of the vein of gold that is your wisdom-nature? How do you know if you are forgetting about serving humanity? You need a navigation device, something to remind you of where you stand and where you are going. You need a spiritual GPS. GPS stands for Global Positioning System, a coordinated array of earth-orbiting satellites that send signals to GPS receivers on earth. With a hand-held GPS receiver, you can tell exactly where you are on the planet at any given moment. In the same way, Buddhist texts provide us with a schema for looking at where we are on the spiritual path and where we are headed. The spiritual journey is sometimes described from three perspectives: Ground, Path, and Summit. We can use these perspectives on the spiritual path to get a bird's-eye view of our day-to-day activities.

The Ground of the spiritual journey is your wisdom-nature, the innate potential and desire to awaken. Gampopa, a great Buddhist master of the twelfth century, said: "Earnest desire to achieve enlightenment is like the earth, because it is the basis for all spiritual qualities." Looking at the spiritual path from the point of view of your wish to achieve enlightenment—or from the point of view of your spiritual intention, whatever that is—reminds you of what the whole mountain stands on. Your intention is like the mirror of your wisdom-nature, what your wisdom-nature would say right now if it could talk. Being mindful of the intention centers you in your overall purpose for being here. It focuses your mind on the big picture.

The Path of the spiritual journey includes all the ways your wisdom-nature is awakened and developed. All the meditations, contemplations, and exercises in this book are part of the Path. The Path is life-intention in practice. In the Buddhist tradition, when the life-intention is moved into action, it is called "the *applied* awakening intention." If your intention is to serve humanity, then the Path is all the little things you think, say, and do to make that intention a reality. Being mindful of the Path means asking yourself, *What will I do today to put my life-intention into action?* and, *In what way am I serving that intention right now?* Those questions are both your motivators and your litmus test with which to measure your actions.

The Summit is the fruition of your intention. It is the culmination of your spiritual journey, the top of the mountain, awakening or enlightenment itself. In one way, the Summit seems far away, but think about it like this. A mountain climber anticipates how elated he or she will feel upon reaching the summit of the mountain in order to find the energy to keep moving up the trail. In that way, think about how free you will feel when your wisdom-nature—your most authentic self—is awakened and fully blossoming.

The spiritual path is not always easy or comfortable. But if you think about how you will feel when humanity is being served in the way you envision it, that gives you a boost of adrenaline for your spiritual journey. It keeps you from overlooking that fruition as it begins to occur in small ways, as you see your actions take root in the world. There are lots of little summits with great views along the way!

So when you are feeling lost and uncertain, take out the tool of the sage's GPS: recall the Ground, the Path, and the Summit. Remembering the *ground* of your wisdom-nature and intention, the *path* of methods to awaken the wisdom-nature, and the *summit* of awakening itself helps you stay on track, develop confidence, and remain focused.

Remember that no aspirations or intentions are written in stone. As you make efforts to deepen your aspirations, they will evolve. Your intention will become more refined. What is important is to have an intention and some aspirations in place. Then your life experience will be the editor! Stasis is not a quality of the spiritual journey; that is one of the reasons why it is an adventure.

Exercise for Day Seven

Contemplating the Sage's GPS

In a quiet place, free from distractions, take a few minutes to contemplate the Ground, your wisdom-nature. Were there times today you felt closer to it? More distant from it?

Now take a minute to think about the Path. Recall your life-intention. Is this the first time today you thought about it? Have you acted on it today consciously, unconsciously?

Take a minute to think about the Summit. This means projecting a bit into the future. How will it feel when you fully realize your wisdom-nature while carrying out loving intentions? Visualize what that will be like for you.

Dharma Tip

Every week in this book ends with a prayer. Use these prayers to augment your spiritual practice. You can cut them out or copy them to use at the end of your contemplation and meditation sessions.

Day Seven

May I embrace life as a spiritual adventure, befriend the
sage's intention, and become a servant of humanity.
Through cultivation of deep prayer, may I be a force of
peace and balance in the world.
May my aspirations for myself and those of all beings come to fruition.

This small nook of mine, my rocky cave,
Is a small place for meditation and reciting prayers.
There is no rain, no snow, no bad things here—
They are cut short by this one-cornered cave.
                              —The hermitess Orgyen Chokyi

Week Three

Create a Sacred Space

Step three is to create a sacred space, a place of retreat and inspiration where you can go to meditate, contemplate, and pray.

One of my teachers, Kalu Rinpoche, used to call himself the Vagrant. There was a reason for this nickname. When he was just twenty-two and living in eastern Tibet, he retreated to the fastness of a mountain cave to practice meditation, much to the consternation of his mother. While other young monks were eating meat and yogurt and drinking butter tea in the monasteries, Kalu Rinpoche was subsisting on boiled nettles and wild berries. While other young men were socializing with the ladies, Kalu Rinpoche preferred the company of rodents, birds, and gazelles.

Eventually, nomads grazing their yaks in the high summer pastures caught on that there was a yogi in their locale. The presence of a cave yogi anywhere in Tibet had a way of attracting the locals. They began to seek him out for guidance and teachings. Monks, nuns, pilgrims, his own family members, and all manner of curious folk began to show up outside his cave.

What is a yogi to do? Rinpoche had withdrawn to the mountains in the first place to seek solitude for meditation, but now he was surrounded by a small community of pilgrims. He tried to ask for solitude, but they would not leave him in peace. So one day, Rinpoche just left unexpectedly, not telling anyone where he was headed. This worked for a few months, but his new cave was eventually discovered. He again snuck out—this time in the middle of the night—to find yet another hermitage. In this way, Rinpoche passed twelve years of his life, retreating to ever-more-remote caves. For that reason, he earned the nickname the Vagrant.

When my own life is unsettled, I take heart thinking about my teacher's early life. Rinpoche gave up his attachment to any one place in favor of finding the right conditions to sustain his spiritual practice. Once he found a good place, he consecrated it with his prayers and meditation. Likewise, when embarking on a spiritual journey, you never know where you will end up. But you can count on your body as your temple, a sacred space you can take anywhere. Wherever you show up prayerful and serene, that place is consecrated as a sacred space.

Day One

Finding a Place of Refuge

*I love to be alone. I never found the companion that was so
companionable as solitude.*

—Henry David Thoreau

Today's Date: _____

By the time I moved into the monastery in 1987, I had encountered
a number of Buddhist teachers who, at one time or another,
meditated in caves. As I listened to their tales of living off nettle
soup, sleeping with bats overhead, and the adventures of leakproofing
a sod roof, I developed a hunger to sample cave meditation. I expressed
this wish to the Buddhist abbot of the monastery where I lived. I even
asked if I might gather stones and mortar them into a hillside to simulate
a cave dwelling. Never mind that this was upstate New York, where the
freezing winters and humid summers were not kind to the best-built
structures.

"Is living in a cave really going to improve your meditation?" the
abbot asked. I could tell he was not waiting on my answer. "I know
someplace just as quiet, dark, and small, and almost as cold!"

The abbot's stout form took up the entire doorway of my tiny room
in the barn. As I peered over his shoulder, he pointed out the various
rearrangements that might be made to accommodate a meditation box,
a traditional Tibetan meditation seat consisting of a wooden frame with
three low sides and a backrest. He stacked up my wooden crates as a
shrine. He suggested some traditional Tibetan implements that I might
acquire whose names I scribbled down judiciously. He even put a stone
on the shrine from a cave where he had meditated in India. *So,* I thought
when he was finished, *a meditation place does not have to be dark, cool,*

89

and earth smelling to be sacred. It does not have to be in the Himalayas. That day I learned that sacred spaces can be created. Once I built my meditation box, I came to perceive it—along with my shrine—as a base camp for spiritual practice, a place of refuge I returned to daily to recharge my batteries.

The simplest kind of spaces can be made sacred. One of my students told me that her sacred space consists of a blanket folded square in the corner of her dorm room. I knew a Buddhist student who was a contractor by trade. He salvaged pieces of cabinet torn out from upscale apartments and reformed them into a shrine that covered an entire wall of his apartment. I know a Buddhist prison chaplain who created a sacred space for her meditation group from an empty, unused cell. For many people, sacred space is as vast as the great outdoors—the beach, the mountains, or a vast desert. For some, it is as small as a portable locket; many lamas I know carry a sacred amulet or locket, known as a *gao*, when they travel that creates a kind of tiny sacred space around the body of the person who carries it.

You have the power to put the *sacred* in sacred space. Sacred spaces are born from an aura of serenity. You can endow your simple meditation spot with such an aura. How? Let us begin with memory. Think back over your life to some place that was a peaceful oasis for you, away from the complications of ordinary life, a place that changed you for the better—a place that made you feel at one with yourself, at one with the universe. What comes to mind for me are some places from my childhood: a favorite climbing tree, a hidden meadow, a hayloft in a horse barn in Montana. Other sacred places from later in my life include the Vatican in Rome, Swayambu Temple in Kathmandu, the gardens in a Franciscan monastery in New York, the Lake of the Goddess's Soul in Tibet. What these places have in common for me is how I felt there: a sense of awe, smallness, and serenity, all at the same time.

What are some of the places in your life that evoke calm or serenity when you merely think of them? In what places in your life have you felt serene and moved, inspired and renewed?

Day One

Creating a sacred space in your dwelling can be a powerful support for your spiritual practice. Your practice of meditation may well rub off on this place, so look for the place or corner you can imagine as a little oasis in your own home. Sometime today, wander around your house or apartment (or dorm room or wherever you live) and feel the spaces there. If you have a garden or other outbuildings, you should check them out as well. Once you find a place that seems suitable, be satisfied with that. There is an old Tibetan saying:

Wherever here is, that is the perfect place to meditate.
Whenever now is, that is the perfect time to meditate.

Even the most humble meditation spot is not only acceptable—it is perfect. Once you find your perfect meditation spot, stand or sit there for a few minutes. Breathe. Feel the space. Arrive there, in your sacred space, with your body, breath, and mind.

A traditional meditation spot has three discrete areas that serve three important functions: a seat, a table, and a shrine. The seat is for you to sit on when you meditate and contemplate. The table is for tools: your reading materials, prayers, and comfort items to support your meditation. The shrine holds sacred objects that uplift and inspire you. Once you arrange these three simple areas, you have the physical conditions in place to sustain a regular contemplative practice over the long run.

Week Three

Exercise for Day One

Find a Sacred Space

- Walk around your home or spaces outdoors.
- Look for a place that you can envision as a spiritual oasis.
- Consider the light. Do you feel better in a well-lighted place or in a place that has little light? Do you want to be by a window?
- Where would you sit in this place? Do you think you would prefer facing a wall or facing away from the wall?
- Consider the sources of noise and activity near this space. Is it fairly quiet? If you have children, is it away from their activity?
- Is the temperature in this space appropriate for your physical comfort?
- Consider the amount of space: can you sit there with a small table?
- Consider the noise and activity level.
- When you have found your sacred space, stand or sit there for a few minutes.
- Practice the Three Arrivals.

Day Two

Adorning Your Space

By Allah! I long to escape the prison of my ego and lose myself in the mountains and the desert.

—Rumi

Today's Date: _____

My first Buddhist meditation teacher, who happened to be a German monk, told me a funny story about his first experience leading a meditation retreat at Kopan monastery near Kathmandu. He was walking around the grounds of the monastery the day before the retreat, getting to know the place. When he passed the shrine room, he noticed a couple of young monks hammering away on an elevated platform at the back of the room. As he approached, he realized they must be preparing the teaching podium that he would sit on the next day. He caught sight of some fine silk brocade lying near the podium ready to cover the wood. He felt himself swell with self-satisfaction. This must be an indication, he thought, that he really had graduated to the status of meditation teacher.

"Hey!" he said cheerfully to one of the carpenters. "Are you making that seat for *me*?"

The young monk looked up and grinned. "No, not for you! We are making this seat for the dharma!"

The monk meant that he was making the seat for the teaching and the spiritual journey itself, not the teacher; for the larger vision of a path, not the traveler. In the same way, as you create your sacred space, know that it is for your life-intention and the good of others, not for only you, the lonely meditator. It is for the whole spiritual journey and by extension for those you serve—for humanity. While setting up your seat, pray for everyone. When you first sit on it, meditate for everyone. If you make it comfortable and pleasing to your eye, offer its comfort and beauty to everyone.

The seat can be a chair, a bench, or a floor cushion. It matters that you can sit there comfortably for some time. These days, meditation and yoga catalogs sell all kinds of meditation seats. If you go online, you can find an array of choices, from firm cushions stuffed with cotton batting, to inflatable travel pillows, to Japanese kneeling benches. It may take you a little time to find a seat you like. I have used everything at some time or other. The important thing is not to delay the creation of your sacred space because you cannot find the perfect seat. Use whatever you have, and you can always change it later.

Now place the seat in your sacred space. Leave room in front or next to you for a small table to hold books and other reading materials you will need, like your Awakening Prayer. I once used an old shoebox for this purpose. Shoeboxes are nice because you can also store things inside, like tissues and lip balm, the staples of serious meditators. These days, at home, I have a low meditation table with a cubby underneath to keep such things.

Next, make a shrine. A shrine is a repository for objects of inspiration. It is a material expression of your spiritual quest. It is a physical space housing symbols that remind you of your commitment to humanity, your community, or the earth, in whatever form that takes for you. These symbols can range from very personal to universal. Symbols are powerful. They speak to us in a language beyond words, and they evoke with imagery. Shrine symbols are selected to remind us of the qualities of wisdom-nature and the spiritual journey.

Start with a surface. Almost any elevated surface will do. Here are some improvisations I have made in my life: a small table, a shelf, the top of a dresser, a box covered with a cloth, a fireplace mantle, a smooth stone, and a board across two cinderblocks, covered with a cloth. For a three-year retreat, we were each supplied with a real Tibetan-style shrine with three levels and cabinet doors. This is a nice luxury if you are a carpenter or have the means to purchase a shrine. But if not, there are many options. It should be visible from your seat but does not have to be near it.

The heart of a shrine is the sacred objects that go in or on it. Start simple. Select what goes on the shrine by how meaningful it feels to you with regard to your spiritual journey. In other words, what you put on your shrine should be a symbolic reflection of your intention and aspirations. Shrine objects are there to uplift or inspire you. Anything that moves you to feel loving, content, and peaceful belongs on a shrine. Especially look for whatever reminds you of your wisdom-nature, the innate potential that you carry with you.

To start with, collect things from around your own home or use natural objects from your yard or other outdoor places. See how creative you can be with what you already have. If that means putting only one object on your shrine, or even visualizing something in front of you, that is enough to start!

In 1959, when the Chinese invaded eastern Tibet, many Tibetans were placed in concentration camps. One of my teachers was in a camp for six months before he escaped. They took everything away from him and his fellow prisoners: his monk's robes, his rosary, his sacred texts—everything. He had only a Chinese uniform provided by the camp wardens. My friend used visualization and what little he had at his disposal. With no outer supports, he continued to visualize his spiritual mentors above his head, and he put aside small bits of food as symbolic offerings to them. When the guards were not looking, he would dip his finger in his drinking water and flick it into the air as a symbolic offering to the Buddha. When the lights went out at night, he sat up in meditation. He had to be covert about his spiritual practices because the Chinese guards punished any religious expression. He told me that the period of six months in a concentration camp was the best retreat he ever had. So while objects can be inspiring and supportive, they are never as important as your mindset and intention. Objects are optional, but intention is essential.

On a Buddhist shrine, you will typically find representations of the Buddha's body, speech, and mind: a statue, a book, and a stupa. Body, speech, and mind are sometimes called the "three gates to liberation" in Buddhist sources, because—when you think about it—that is precisely where liberation is going to take place: in your body, speech, and mind (and the bodies, speeches, and minds of everyone else). The physical, verbal, and mental aspects of your being are like the clay you have to work with. Awakening can be fashioned out of nothing else. Therefore, it makes sense that the most basic objects on a shrine represent body, speech, and mind in their awakened or perfected form, because that is where we aspire to go.

The statue—the symbol of awakened body—might be of the Buddha, or it might be of some other enlightened being. It is intended to communicate that enlightenment takes form in the world through action. The book represents awakened speech and the many ways the spiritual path can be expressed through verbal teachings. A stupa—representing awakened mind—is a small reliquary that comes in a few shapes, usually being a carved mound or thick spire with bas relief designs. When the Buddha died, his ashes were placed in such a reliquary, and it is believed that those relics still survive. So ever after, the shape of the stupa came to be associated with the Buddha's undying wisdom-mind.

If you want, you can look for symbolic representations of awakened body, speech, and mind in your own home (or these days, online). Choose objects or images that are personally meaningful. As a representation of awakened body, a statue of the Buddha is not the most meaningful image for everyone. It might be a picture of your spiritual mentor, an image of a person to whom you feel devotion, or something else entirely. On my first shrine, I placed a painting of the Virgin Mary and Jesus that I found at a garage sale as a kid, because it reminded me of the power of motherly love. Later, it was the image of Tara. Then these were joined by a Buddha statue. A shrine can be a work in progress.

The question to ask yourself is, *What reminds me of the potential of my body and the bodies of everyone to become sages?* The body is the vessel that carries you to awakening. What reminds you that your own body and the bodies of others are precious vessels? What reminds you that your body is an instrument of carrying out your life-intention?

The body is your sacred temple, the most sacred of spaces, where awakening occurs. What reminds you that your body is a crucible for enlightenment? Some examples of representations of body include photos of inspiring people who have used their bodies to inspire and uplift others, statues, body images, or an object that reminds you of your body's potential. I have seen someone use a small cactus. When I asked her why the cactus, she replied, "It is like me . . . spiny on the outside, and soft on the inside! It reminds me to look for the softness in myself."

For the representation of speech, the question to ask is, *What reminds me of the potential of my speech, and the speech of all people, to become enlightened?* Your speech is the instrument of communication with the world. It is through speech that the mind's wisdom and love translates into words that inspire and uplift others. The vehicle of language and speech is the reason we are able to traverse a path at all and is the conduit of teaching and learning. Some traditional representations of awakened speech include sacred books or texts, inspiring poetry, rosaries or prayer beads (symbolizing the repetition of a set of empowering syllables called a mantra), bells, chimes, drums, and conch shells. Almost anything that makes a pleasant sound could be a representation of awakened speech. In the Tibetan Buddhist environment, even the alphabet (and every letter of the alphabet) is considered inherently sacred, because it is the vehicle of the communication of sound and meaning and is sometimes repeated during prayers to bless a person's speech. These days, a representation of awakened speech could even be a CD.

For the representation of mind, the question to ask yourself is, *What reminds me of the potential of my mind—my innermost wisdom-nature—to awaken?* Although the wisdom-nature has no form, if you had to give it a form, what would you choose? The Buddhists tradition-ally use a stupa. You could choose whatever reminds you of your mind's potential to awaken perfect love and wisdom. Some traditional Tibetan representations of the mind include a crystal, because mind refracts the light of truth as many colors; a mirror, because all sense appearances are reflected in the surface of awareness; a jewel or *vajra*, because the mind is indestructible; and a sword, as a symbol that a sage's wisdom cuts through everything else. These are just a few. Think about what kind of symbol works for you. You do not have to limit yourself to traditional images.

Exercise for Day Two

Adorn Your Sacred Space

Find a comfortable seat, cushion, or chair. Make a shrine beside or in front of your seat, where you can see it; any elevated surface will do.

Place on it any object that inspires you or reminds you of your life-intention; or you could place one thing that reminds you of awakened body, one thing that reminds you of awakened speech, and one thing that reminds you of awakened mind.

Put a small utility table or box by your seat.

Day Three

Offerings and Inauguration

We are not here to curse the darkness; we are here to light a candle.

—John F. Kennedy

Today's Date: _____

Now that you have set up the representations on your shrine, you may want to offer something to them. What is offering? In effect, offering is an act of *honoring*. By offering to the representations of awakened body, speech, and mind, you honor all aspects of your spiritual journey from the ground to the summit. First you honor the *ground* of awakening: the wisdom-nature in yourself and all living beings, the awakening potential of body, speech, and mind. One way to think of this is that you are making an offering to, and honoring, the spiritual community of seekers.

Second, you honor the *path* of awakening. You offer to awakening as a process: to the unfolding of perfection in the body, speech, and mind of yourself and others. Honoring the path strengthens your commitment to the spiritual journey and all its permutations.

Finally, you honor the *summit* of awakening. Traditional sources would call this an offering to the Buddha. You honor the body, speech, and mind in its already awakened state. Put another way, you are looking at the summit of the quest and making an offering to models of awakened perfection. If you are of a devotional disposition, you can mentally dedicate your offerings to those spiritual heroes whom you take as spiritual guides: people you admire or teachers who inspire you. If not, you can dedicate your offerings to an ideal of perfect love and wisdom; you do not have to give it a form. Dedicate your offerings to what you aspire to, what you serve, and who you are in your heart of hearts.

Dharma Tip

The ritual of making an offering to your shrine can become a daily practice. For example, light a candle on your shrine before meditating, or offer a cup of tea. Tibetan Buddhists fill seven water bowls on their shrines every morning to begin the day with an act of devotion.

What do you offer? In general, offerings can be anything that pleases your senses. Traditional offerings include candles, incense, flowers, musical instruments (such as bells), food, water, and soft, beautiful cloth such as silk. Water is convenient because, while flowers and so forth might be hard to get, water almost never is.

One of my favorite offerings is a candle or some other offering of light.

When you meditate, you light up the world with your spiritual aspirations, instead of dismissing the world as a shadowy place beyond your control. In Buddhist sources, a candle symbolizes sometimes the incandescence of wisdom, sometimes the guiding light of love. It also creates an ambience for peace, a pleasant glow in the room.

The candle flame is sometimes used as a focus for meditation. Try resting your gaze on the steady light of your shrine candle while you relax into meditation. Think of it as a symbol of the steady light of your wisdom-nature. This is a method that was used and taught by Milarepa, one of the most famous yogis in the history of Tibet. He used a lamp made of butter from a *dri*, a female yak. Once he placed the lamp on his head for a long time to keep himself awake and alert during meditation. If he lost his concentration and nodded off, the melted butter sloshed onto his head, a quick and efficient wake-up call!

Day Three

Exercise for Day Three
Inaugurate Your Sacred Space

- Make an offering to the representations on your shrine (examples: a candle, flowers, a bowl of clear water).
- As you do so, recall the meaning of the offering; mentally honor the ground, path, and summit of your spiritual journey.
- Sit in your sacred space. Practice the Three Arrivals.
- Recite your Awakening Prayer. Pray deeply.

Day Four

Inspirational Material

Inspiration is God making contact with itself.

—Ram Dass

Today's Date: _____

O nce you have designed and inaugurated your meditation
space, you may want to acquire a few additional inspirational
materials to keep there. Reading materials are a good place to
start. What in this book has piqued your interest? What quotations or
ideas? What poems, biographies, and stories have inspired you in the
past? Resurrect some of these, or seek out new ones.

These days, thanks to the Internet, it is very easy to reach out and
find reading material, either online or by ordering books. Sure, it is
possible to stumble onto material that is misleading, but let being
misled and confused motivate you to search until you gain a wider
understanding. Reading is good to broaden your knowledge and to cull
inspiration for your quest from all the many sources that are available.
You can keep some of this material on the little table or shoebox by
your shrine and read a passage or two now and then while sitting in
your sacred space.

But do not limit yourself to reading: what images inspire you? I first
became attracted to Tibetan Buddhism when I saw a Tibetan painting
(or *thanka*) of White Tara hanging in a temple in Kathmandu. White
Tara is an enlightened goddess used as a focus in meditation, a kind of
heroine archetype of spiritual perfection. When I first saw that painting,

I was captivated by her eyes—their serene gaze, looking both at and through me—and I wanted to understand more about her. I finally found a picture small enough to photocopy. Just having that image near me when I meditated changed the way I practiced. I looked at her peaceful demeanor and felt the serenity of my meditation deepen. I looked at her eyes and sensed the communication of heroic love through them. Images can be powerfully suggestive of the qualities of awakening. That was the beginning of my interest in Tibetan deity practices, a kind of practice discussed later in this book.

In addition to the representations of body, speech, and mind, you might also gather a few other objects that inspire and uplift your spirit, make you smile, remind you to feel grateful, and warm your heart. There is a famous Tibetan story of a woman whose son brought her a gift of a dog's tooth for her shrine, telling her that it was actually the tooth of the Buddha. Even though the object was nothing but a tooth yanked from the skull of a dead dog, she did not know that, so she was filled with inspiration and devotion every time she looked at the tooth. Eventually, she prayed so hard and with such devotion to the tooth that—to everyone's surprise—she traversed the whole spiritual path and attained awakening. So any object can be sacred: a sacred object is made so by how you see it and how you use it. Some of my favorite shrine objects come from beautiful outdoor places I have visited that remind me of peace and serenity (sea shells, stones, pressed flowers) or from pilgrimage spots I have visited.

Exercise for Day Four

Finishing Touches

Acquire/order/download an inspirational book, picture, or poem. Personalize your shrine. Make it sacred to you. Look for things that

- inspire
- uplift
- put the heart at peace
- make you feel grateful
- warm your heart
- are sacred to you

Day Five

Plumbing the Wisdom-Nature through Introspection

In solitude the mind gains strength and learns to lean upon itself.
—Laurence Sterne

Today's Date: _____

Now that you have set up a sacred space, you are ready to expand your meditation practice. Last week, you created an Awakening Prayer made up of an intention and aspirations. You focused on where you want to go and the people in your life who point the way. You now have a broad idea of where you are going on this spiritual journey. But how will you know, at any given time, if you are on track? How will you know when you are doing the right thing? What will be the clue or set of clues that lets you know?

There is a short answer to the question. A sage cultivates two main character traits. The whole repertoire of tools in the sage's toolkit are for tuning up these two traits, in one way or another. These traits are *wisdom* and *love*: the double doors to awakening. Wisdom and love reveal the clues to right action. I say "double doors" because these two character traits always go together. The Buddha said that one without the other is like a bird with a broken wing. Only when the wings of wisdom and love both work will the bird of enlightenment fly. Love without wisdom is like a blind person leading the blind. Wisdom without love is like gold hiding in quartz. Wisdom gives the blind eyes, and love makes the gold of the world shine.

How do these two traits help us discover wisdom-nature? Wisdom helps you know your deepest nature and tap into the qualities that express it. Wisdom also helps you discriminate between help and what might bring harm. Love, on the other hand, helps you *feel* your deepest nature and tap into the ocean of love there. Through developing compassion, you learn to *feel* intuitively what the right thing to do is. Through knowing and feeling, you awaken the enlightened qualities of a sage. Therefore, the Buddhist tradition offers many contemplations and meditations, methods of introspection aimed at developing love and wisdom—initially by turns and eventually simultaneously.

Introspective practices that deepen wisdom and love are helped by taking an interlude of seclusion, silence, and mental solitude. I call these the *Three S's*. In meditation texts, they are sometimes referred to as isolation of body, isolation of speech, and isolation of mind. *Isolation* does not necessarily mean withdrawing to a place where no other people exist. It means setting aside a period of time in the day, even for a few minutes, to be alone with the central support for your spiritual journey: yourself.

Seclusion refers to finding space and time, however short, to move your body out of its usual busyness. It can mean taking a miniretreat into your sacred space or creating a mental protection circle around your body for a short time. If you work in an office, for instance, this can even be done on a coffee break.

Seclusion means physically relaxing and taking time out from physical movement, as much as possible. I say "as much as possible" because for some people it is literally not possible to be physically still. I once met a meditator with Parkinson's disease, a degenerative disease of the nervous system. She was a proficient meditator even though her body was never completely still.

I asked her once about this and she said, "My body does its own thing. It is what thought is to other meditators. Some people cannot control their thoughts. In my case, I cannot control my body. But, like anyone else, I can still find equilibrium." What she meant is that, when she meditates, the movement of her body is no longer disturbing. She finds stillness within movement, in the same way that a meditator discovers stillness within the occurrence of thought. The art of entering seclusion is the art of discovering stillness. In time, you will get into the groove of discovering peace right within the colorful backdrop of whatever presents itself to your senses.

Silence means taking a break from the habit of speech. It means dropping conversation. It also means taking time out from the sound of speech, music, and noise that surrounds so many people at home and at work these days: all those sounds that issue constantly from the TV, radio, and iPod. I am amazed at how many people fail to enjoy silence each day. I think I am amazed because of all the good it would do them. Some people are afraid of silence, feeling somehow that if the noise stops, they will have to listen to their own thoughts.

But there is nothing to fear and everything to gain from just a few minutes of silence every day. It reconnects you with the peace that lives inside. Consider Mother Teresa's words:

> God is the friend of silence. See how nature—trees, flowers, grass—
> grows in silence; see the stars, the moon, and the sun, how they move
> in silence. . . . We need silence to be able to touch souls.

Silence has its own profound sound. It is the resonance of your true nature, the mood of tranquility, the timbre of inner peace. That sacred, soundless music nourishes the human heart so that we can reach out to serve others.

Solitude, the third *S,* refers to mental solitude. It means taking a break from the busyness of your mind. It means taking a time-out— not just a break but a moment "out of time." Sometimes the meditation texts divide time into three times: past, present, and future. Stepping out of time means dropping your obsession with the past, present, and future.

Try it now. First, let go of your thoughts about what happened last year, last week, yesterday, this morning. Then let go of your anticipation of future events—what you will do later today, tomorrow, next week. Finally, drop your fixations in the present—with that construction going on next door or a backache you have, for instance. When you really let go of the past, future, and present, you enter a timeless moment. Give yourself permission to simply be. Being in this timeless moment is mental solitude, an oasis of mental peace. In meditation texts, this is called the *fourth time*, the time beyond time.

Practicing the Three S's paves the way for the introspective practices of contemplation and meditation. It removes your body, speech, and mind from distractions and establishes the baseline conditions for development of tranquility, deep reflection, and meditation. Just a simple time-out is enough to change you. Dilgo Khyentse Rinpoche, a great Tibetan meditation master of the twentieth century, said:

> Even if inwardly awareness is not clear right now,
> Simply keep the mind from wandering outside;
> This will do, for awareness lies in the very depth of the mind.

Even if pure awareness, the core of your true nature, is not apparent to you right now, establishing the conditions for inner peace is a great stride toward recognizing it. And these conditions do not take days or months to establish. They take only a moment, the moment of finding inner space, the domain of mental solitude.

That moment requires no particular external conditions. So the old excuse, *I do not have time to meditate*, does not fly from the point of view of momentary meditation. Meditation does not have to be a big deal. It is as simple as taking a short break daily—even for one or two minutes—to practice a miniretreat of the Three S's. It might change your life.

Before we go on, it is helpful to distinguish between two types of inner cultivation that we will be working with over the course of these few weeks: *contemplation* and *meditation*. Contemplation develops your innate imaginative voice and your faculty of deep knowing. As a spiritual practice, contemplation is the act of sitting down, relaxing, and probing deeply into a subject. Instead of treating something in a shallow and cursory way, you allow lots of time for looking at the subject from every angle. Contemplating includes questioning, probing, and imagining. These are the activities of contemplation. If you do this in a peaceful place, with your body and breathing relaxed, you will discover that you already have an inner wisdom capable of probing life's most difficult questions. Love, patience, gratitude, courage, and many other positive character traits can be strengthened through imaginative contemplation.

Meditation develops concentration, tranquility, and wisdom. The faculty of wisdom helps you effectively implement your aspirations and intentions: you need wisdom to understand how to make your values, wishes, and dreams manifest in the real world. There are many kinds of meditation, but all Buddhist forms of meditation aim to awaken the inner wisdom-nature. Initially, meditation helps you develop the mental space for wisdom to emerge on its own. Later, meditation training involves developing mental skills to cut through confusion, distraction, and other barriers. And finally, meditation makes full awakening possible.

Generally, meditation is a two-step process of (1) working with techniques to calm the mind and (2) working with techniques to catalyze an experience of direct insight into the mind's nature. Direct insight is the experience of an initial glimpse of your deepest nature, your truest self. It is followed by a process of stabilizing or "getting used to" that insight and eventually making it a part of your conscious experience at all times. This week's meditation is along the lines of the first step, calming the mind.

Before you contemplate or meditate, you may want to make time and space. Find a time when you can spend a few minutes in relative peace and quiet. If you use your sacred space, that is good. When you cannot use your usual spot, take space where you can get it. When even that space is less than ideal, you can create a peaceful space around your own body by visualizing yourself in a translucent crystal-like bubble made of light. This bubble is called a *protection circle*, and it is used in some Buddhist practices to create a place of peace, relaxation, and safety. Imagining such a bubble around your body is an effective mental technique to limit distractions and keep peace of mind in.

Exercise for Day Five

The Three S's

Practice seclusion. Move your body to a place where you are alone and away from interaction.

Practice silence. Turn off all sources of sound around you. Enjoy the silence.

Practice solitude. Drop thoughts about the past and future. Enter into the timeless present, the fourth time. Give yourself permission simply to be, and enjoy your own company.

This whole process need take only five or ten minutes.

Day Six

Breath Meditation

Act as if what you do makes a difference. It does.

—William James

Today's Date: _____

When we need a vacation, we have no trouble taking one. But how often do we give our most important instrument, the mind, a real rest? How often do we take the time to slow down and calm the mind? Yet how dependent we are on it! When we need rest, we have no trouble resting the body. One of the functions of meditation is to give the mind the vacation it deserves. Meditation is a profound way of reducing stress, increasing well-being, and, most important, making space for wisdom to emerge on its own.

You do not have to be a genius to learn to meditate. Indeed, one of Milarepa's very first disciples was a teenage shepherd who had never learned to read or write. All he knew how to do was herd sheep. When the boy approached Milarepa for meditation instruction, Milarepa instructed the boy:

> In order to meditate, simply place your mind on the breath, as you inhale and exhale. When you are trying to meditate like that, thoughts will come up. Just act as if you were doing what you do every day as a shepherd. When meditating, you need to cultivate the ability to watch thought, the way a shepherd on a hillside contentedly watches his flock of sheep. Do not let the thoughts drag your attention away from the breath. Do not follow after the thoughts, try to control them, or make them go away. Let them coexist with your meditation on the breath.

With these instructions, the shepherd went off to meditate. He had a lot of experience watching sheep, so the shepherd knew he could focus on something—like mending a harness—while still being aware of the sheep out of the corner of his eye. He tried the same thing with his meditation, befriending thoughts as he would a flock of sheep, while still focusing on the breath. His concentration was so good, the story goes, he lost track of time and remained absorbed in meditation for a week. In the end, this shepherd became one of Milarepa's best disciples and one of the most accomplished meditation masters in Tibet. The point is that what we think of as "intelligence," or intellectual acuity, has little to do with success at meditation.

This week's meditation is called breath meditation, and it is like the meat (or tofu!) of your meditation sandwich. Like the Three Arrivals, breath meditation has no topic to be explored and no analysis. It is a meditation about calming down, focusing, and centering. When done consistently or even occasionally, it has the power to bring peace and balance to your life.

This week you will complete the meditation sandwich. Meditating is not much different from following a cooking recipe. Just as when you are cooking, focus on one step at a time—do not be distracted by the instructions as a whole. Once you know the recipe, you will hardly have to think about it. As in Week One, begin with the Three Arrivals. Then say your Awakening Prayer. You can simply recite it once, aloud, if convenient. The Awakening Prayer reminds you where you are going: it is like looking at the aerial map of your journey so that you remember that this small act of meditating is a step toward your goal.

Now you are ready to meditate. Close your eyes, or lower your gaze. This will help keep you from getting distracted by things in your field of vision. Straighten your posture. This will help keep you alert and will infuse your meditation with a gentle discipline. If you have any physical limitations, you should not worry if you cannot sit straight . . . you can meditate in any posture. These instructions are just general recommendations.

Day Six

Now become aware of the coming and going of breath. Let yourself breathe normally and without effort. Place your attention on the feeling of the breath in your nostrils as you inhale and exhale. Focus your mind on that sensation. You should be neither too tightly focused—trying with effort to force your attention onto the feeling—nor too loose—spacing out and forgetting the feeling of the breath. The Buddha once described it to a sitar player as being like properly tuning a sitar, a type of Indian stringed instrument. If you pull the string too tightly, it will break. If you leave it too loose, it will not make a good sound. Similarly, you need to get used to an attention that focuses on the breath with the right balance between tightness, or concentration, and looseness, or relaxation.

If thoughts arise, allow them to come and go, like waves rising and falling back into the ocean, or like Milarepa's shepherd disciple who watched his thoughts like sheep. If you get distracted from watching the breath, do not be overly concerned about it. Just return your attention to the breath when you notice the distraction. You may find you have to do this many times in a session. It is normal to get distracted often in the beginning. That is why, in the Tibetan meditation tradition, the first phase of meditation is called "like a waterfall." Thoughts seem to come in a steady stream. Over time, the waterfall becomes more like a slowly moving river. Finally it becomes like a great, calm ocean. Meditate in this way for five to ten minutes.

Exercise for Day Six
Breath Meditation

- The Three Arrivals: Arrive with body, breath, and mind.
- Say your Awakening Prayer aloud.
- Close your eyes or lower your gaze. Straighten your spine and relax.
- Become aware of the coming and going of breath.
- Place your mind on the feeling of the breath in your nostrils as the air passes in and out. Focus your mind on that sensation.
- If thoughts arise, allow them to come and go, like waves rising and falling back into the ocean. Keep returning your attention to the breath.
- Meditate for five to ten minutes.

Day Seven

Dedication

What is a hero without love for mankind?
                                    —Doris Lessing

Today's Date: _____

*I*n the beginning of most books, there is a dedication to a person or persons. You have doubtless seen TV episodes or movies dedicated to someone. Spiritual sages also make dedications, but instead of dedicating a work of art, they dedicate their spiritual practice.

Dedication of your practice comes at the end of a spiritual activity to reinforce the connection between your inner work and its ultimate goal. You dedicate to the *fulfillment of a purpose.* By mentally sealing an activity, such as your contemplation, with such a dedication, you ensure that the energy and time you spend goes toward the fulfillment of your life-intention and aspirations.

In Week One, your purpose was to begin discovering your wisdom-nature. For Week Two, you developed a life-intention and aspirations. So the dedication—the summing up of your practice—seals your journey of discovery and your life-intention in some way. Here is one Dedication Prayer I sometimes use as an example:

This contemplation [or meditation] is dedicated to the awakening of my wisdom-nature for the good of the world and all beings within it.

But why not compose a Dedication Prayer in your own words? If you were to dedicate your meditation to something, what would it be?

Dedication is the final piece of bread on your sandwich. Keep it handy with your Awakening Prayer. While the meat of your practice will change, the Three Arrivals, the Awakening Prayer, and the Dedication are staples. To review, your meditation sandwich looks like this:

1. Three Arrivals: Arrive in the here and now.

2. Awakening Prayer: Chant, recite, or read your prayer.

3. Meditation or contemplation: Follow the instructions for the meditation or contemplation at hand. The key to success in this phase is relaxation and focus.

4. Dedication: Chant, pray, recite, or read your dedication.

Tranquility meditation, sometimes called *mindfulness meditation*, of which breath meditation is one variety, is the foundation for most other meditation practices. This form of meditation, practiced by Eastern religions for thousands of years, has been validated by scientific studies to reduce stress, increase pain tolerance, enhance well-being, increase brain size and function, and improve physical health. Medical clinics use it as a stress-reduction therapy. There is almost no reason not to do it. However, for a spiritual seeker, those are byproducts to a more profound goal. The most important aspect of meditation is that it brings you closer to the wisdom-nature; it increases clarity of mind.

The effects of tranquility meditation are cumulative. You may notice soon after starting a meditation practice that your mind is changing. You might feel as if you are beginning to get in touch with a part of yourself long forgotten. Other effects of meditation take time to emerge. The important thing is not to have expectations before, during, or after meditation. Instead, use your meditation time to learn to relax deeply and let go. When you let go, your wisdom-nature comes forward on its own. Remember, learning to relax is a *skill*, developed through repetition. Once you develop it, life becomes much easier, and you find a new sense of spaciousness and clarity of mind. If you have time, continue to do this meditation daily, until you receive the instructions for next week's meditation practice.

Why is clarity of mind useful? One reason is that clarity of mind gives you the space to notice whether what you do every day is reflecting your intention and aspirations. The more you become aware that your actions are reflecting your intention and aspirations, the more excited you will become about life. When you serve a noble intention, one that you feel good about, your actions take on greater meaning, and life becomes a challenge. How will you take the circumstances you are given today to serve your life-intention? You will begin to see life the way mountaineers see a mountain, or the way skiers see the downhill slope, or the way racers see the track. The fun is not in reaching the goal, but in the process of getting there. Life becomes a challenge, and its twists and turns become like moguls on a slope. You cannot wait to meet them.

Exercise for Day Seven

Compose a Dedication Prayer (or Two)

When I meditate, I would like to dedicate my meditation to the fulfillment of the following goals:

_____

_____

_____

My Dedication Prayer(s):

_____

_____

_____

_____

Day Seven

May I treasure sacred space in my life.
May I commune daily with seclusion, silence, and solitude.
May all inner work contribute to my mission to awaken
and inspire others to love and serve the human family.

Just as a mother will risk her life
To love and protect her only child,
A sage cultivates boundless love
For everything that lives throughout the universe.
                                        — The Buddha

Week Four

Grow Love

Step four is to grow love. This week you will awaken your innate capacity for universal love and experiment with ways to develop that capacity.

A spiritual journey takes courage and vision at the outset, but to sustain such courage and vision you need fuel: a love that is correspondingly courageous and visionary. You need a heart without borders. What ideology, a mere set of beliefs, is strong enough to drive the spiritual journey upward and onward for a lifetime? Only true feeling, directed to all humanity, is strong enough to do that. If there is an energy bar for your spiritual journey, it would be universal love. But universal love is not something you will find in the future; you can find the seed for universal love by looking close to home, at your own heart and experience just as it is.

Day One

Love Considered

Loving compassion is the electricity of spiritual practice. If it is cut, nothing works anymore.

—Bokar Rinpoche

Today's Date: _____

*W*hat is your relationship to the word *love*? How do you define it? What is the scope of your love? Do you reserve your love for some and withhold it from others? Who and why? We have all experienced love, but our relationship with the word fluctuates, depending on the context or on our personal history as we remember it at the moment. Some of my favorite songs on the radio are love songs—they are so easy to relate to. What a window they are into the spectrum of how we define love and how we all have thought about love some of the time. Even the titles! Think of Steve Winwood's plea for a "Higher Love," Freddy Mercury caught up in that "Crazy Little Thing Called Love," Joan Baez bitterly lamenting that "Love Is Just a Four-Letter Word."

One thing seems certain: the definition of love is subjective, and it colors how we see the world. Your relationship to the word *love* is therefore worth examining. Jot down your definition of love or a list of things you think of when you think of love. Do not worry—you will not be married to this definition! It is just a proposal. It is the thought process that is illuminating. Begin with *Love is...* and come up with some words that capture the essence of love. It should come from your heart and be based on what you really feel, not what you think you should feel. Your understanding of love is not necessarily the same as the next person's. Reflecting on how you define love at this moment will give you insight into your actions this week and will help you notice when the scope of your love grows.

Exercise for Day One

Defining "Love"

What is your definition of love? Try finishing these sentences:

Love is (list some adjectives) _____

Love is never _____

I find it easy to love _____

My definition of love _____

Day Two

Two Myths about Love

We can't accept others depply until we learn to receive the love that accepts us deeply.

—Lama John Makransky

Today's Date: _____

We all have myths about love. Love myths are stories we tell ourselves about who we are in relation to love. While we may live with others some of the time, we live with ourselves *all* the time. Some of our strongest internal myths are thus tied to our own experiences with love and are rooted not so much in how we relate to others but more in how we perceive ourselves. Whatever relationship you have developed with your own mind and body is going to influence how you relate to others. For that reason, *you cannot effectively accept and love others unless you initially accept and love yourself.*

Loving yourself does not mean developing a self-important attitude. It means recognizing that you, like everyone else, have the potential to awaken, are a sage-at-heart, and are therefore worthy of love. When you recognize that and allow yourself to receive love, it is easy to see the purity in others, widen the scope of your love, and have true humility and compassion. An important part of the spiritual journey, therefore, is gradually to learn to love yourself while simultaneously developing love for others.

One way to do this is to recognize our subliminal myths. Our myths may only be situational, or they might be with us every day. Occasionally it is helpful to look for them and to see what we find. Here and on Day Three, I will focus on four myths that I have noticed over the course of my life and work as a student and teacher. I think that most of us succumb to these myths at least some of the time. Recognizing them helps us rewrite the love storyline and revise the power of love in the light of being on a spiritual journey.

Myth: I do not deserve to be loved.
Truth: Everyone is worthy of love.

Let us suppose you have wisdom-nature. Let us suppose your nature—not your appearance, not your personality, but your most authentic nature—is wisdom. If that is true, no matter what you may have done in life or what kind of person you think you are, you are still indelibly stamped with greatness. You are destined to become a fully enlightened buddha. If you are stamped with such greatness, how could you not be worthy of love?

Asanga, an ancient Buddhist master, put it this way: "[Spiritual potential] is as enduring as space. . . . A corrupt disposition will not damage it, and a pure disposition cannot improve it." If your nature is really as enduring as space, there is nothing you can do to your wisdom-nature to destroy it—just as you could not destroy space if you wanted to. Your potential for good is incorruptible. No matter what you have done or what your personality is like, there is nothing that can alter, shatter, or harm the innate purity that is your wisdom-nature.

On the flip side, no matter how good you might try to become, you cannot make your wisdom-nature any better—*a pure disposition cannot improve it*. It is perfect just as it is. The spiritual path is not about improving your wisdom-nature. It is coming to know fully what you already have. In the same book quoted above, Asanga describes the spiritual path as an allegory. A man is walking on a muddy path one day and drops a nugget of gold. It sits there in the muck for hundreds of years, unchanged and undamaged by the ravages of time.

Then one day a god who can see things clairvoyantly spies the gold, even though it has sunk far into the ground. A man eventually walks down that path, and the god says to him, "Hey! Right at your feet is a nugget of gold. It is all covered with dirt, but you should dig it up and smelt it into some jewelry. Make use of it!" In the same way, a seeker gets a whiff of the presence of the wisdom-nature—the gold deep within. Even though the gold itself is pure, it needs to be mined and refined in order for it to become useful. A seeker strives to uncover it and bring out its innate luster—that is what the spiritual journey is all about.

Because that inner purity is the basis of a spiritual life, there is nothing more worthy or valuable in the world, and it is closer to you than anything else. That is why you are worthy of love. Not loving yourself is like turning your back on the innate purity that is the true nature of yourself and everyone else in the world. It is like leaving the gold nugget in the mud. When you work to become comfortable with receiving love from yourself and others, you honor the presence of wisdom-nature. This is a much more rewarding way to live than resisting love. Without even being fully aware of it, we exhaust ourselves trying to justify why we are not worthy of it.

Trungpa Rinpoche, a Tibetan Buddhist master who came to America in the sixties, pointed out: "The obsession with our own inadequacies is one of the biggest obstacles on the bodhisattva's path." You might diagnose your habits and disposition and conclude you are not perfect. That kind of introspection has its place. You need to notice your dark places, the places you fall short. You need tools and methods to clear the mud obscuring the nugget of inner wisdom. Fashioning the jewelry of enlightenment takes effort.

Dharma Tip

The *Middle Way* is an important concept for Buddhists. Originally, as the Buddha taught it, the term meant that leading a life of balance is the path to wisdom. More specifically, the Buddha taught that it is not wise to be too self-indulgent or too self-denying. Instead, we should live a life of balance. Over the centuries, the term came to apply to a wider meaning of finding a middle ground between extremes and developing a stance of compassionate equanimity.

But we often focus so intently on the mud that we lose sight of the gold. We resort to labels, trying to put a finger on what is wrong with life at the moment: *I am such a difficult/neurotic/depressed person, I am a failure, I am no fun to be around*, and so forth. Instead, we have an option to follow a middle way, recognizing there is work to be done but not losing sight of inner wisdom. Distinguishing the mud from the gold within becomes the basis for truly valuing yourself. You may have imperfections—who does not?—but you are not your imperfections. What would it look like to bring the Middle Way into your life and thought process?

> *Myth: No one ever really loved me or loves me now.*
> *Truth: You have been loved in the past and are loved now.*

When you reflect haplessly on the past—in your darker moments—you might conclude no one has ever really loved you. But if you reflect carefully, you will discover that you have been loved, more often than you know. You will find that sometime in your life, there has been at least one person (and probably many more) who loved you. It might have been a parent, a friend, a sibling, even a pet. He or she may never have said the words "I love you," but you can still recognize the love that was there. How? Because you *felt good* around this person. You felt safe, you felt comfortable. You felt a bond. He or she made gestures or spoke in a manner that made you feel safe and comfortable . . . that was his or her way of expressing love. Such a person, one who helps you recognize you are loved, is called a *benefactor*.

You are also loved now. When you feel completely alone in the world, it can be comforting to know that every sage in the world, now and throughout history, has included you in his or her prayers, prayers motivated by love. I am always excited to unearth a new version of spiritual inclusiveness in the prayers of great beings. Consider this prayer made by Kalu Rinpoche throughout his life:

> For all beings, as numerous as the sky is vast, may love and compassion
> arise from the depths of my heart.

The scope of a sage's love and prayers includes all humanity, not just a small circle of people. Humanity is a family you belong to! The club of a sage's love is not exclusive, not even bound by distance or time. Sages work to extend love to more and more people, even people they have never met. They are willing to go through hell, literally, if it means making life better for just a single person. It is comforting to know that, right now, even as you read these words, someone somewhere loves you that intensely and sincerely. What better gift could we give back to these great beings of the past and present than to recognize their gift of love? Eventually, we may even give them the gift of becoming like them.

The more worthy you feel, the more you discover love has always been around you and is in your life now. Once you discover the pervasiveness of love, you can work on the skill of accepting, receiving, and appreciating love. Keep in mind that learning to accept love from others is not an inherent trait. It is a skill. Over time, the more skillful you become at accepting love, the better you will be at repaying the kindnesses all around you. And what better way to repay someone for loving you than accepting their love?

Exercise for Day Two

Identify Benefactors

Take some time to look back over your life experiences. Who in your life has loved you and cared for you? List just one of these people below. If you think of more, list them too.

My benefactors are

_____

_____

_____

Day Three

Two More Myths about Love

Love is a sacred reserve of energy; it is like the blood of spiritual evolution.

—Teilhard de Chardin

Today's Date: _____

Yesterday we contemplated how not only are we each worthy of love, we *are* loved. Today, we will consider two more myths about love that relate to loving others. In our spiritual practice, love is a two-way street: we benefit from receiving it and giving it.

Myth: Love is something that "happens" to people.
Truth: Love needs to be cultivated.

You cannot just sit back and wait for love to happen to you. If you do, you will probably wait a very long time. You have to work on it! Love is a choice that *sometimes* happens to people. Even when it "happens" to someone, it will quickly "unhappen" without cultivation.

Cultivation means taking steps to grow the seed of love in all areas of your life. A seeker takes a proactive stance to sprouting love and nurturing it. Patrul Rinpoche put it simply:

> It is vital to cultivate [universal love] until it has truly taken root in us. To make things as easy as possible to understand, we can summarize [love and compassion] in the single phrase "a kind heart." Just train yourself to have a kind heart always and in all situations.

This cultivation might start with reflecting on the qualities of wisdom-nature and universal love. It might mean looking for ways to expand

132

your love, such as the ways included here or elsewhere. But be creative. Your training may mean forgiving someone you have a grudge against. The act of forgiving is one direct way to melt parts of yourself that are rigid. So this is your exercise for Day Three. Start with forgiving small harms as an exercise toward forgiving larger harms.

This week, think about how you might soften your hard edges at work and at home. As you read the chapter this week, think about what having a *kind heart* means to you. How can you melt the rigid parts of yourself? How can you make your heart more tender?

> *Myth: I gave everything I had to him/her/it and now I have nothing left to give.*
> *Truth: No matter what your personal history, you are capable of love.*

No matter what your past looks like, no matter what your personal history, you are capable of love. Spiritual biographies are full of examples of people who suffered great loss, or took a wrong turn, and then went on to become exemplary sages, with great love for all humanity.

One such person was the wisdom woman Sukhasiddhi, the tenth-century founder of the Shangpa Buddhist lineage. Sukha (the short form of her name) was living with her husband and two children in a small village in a region of northern India when a great famine swept through the region. One day, when her family was out looking for food, a poor and hungry beggar came to the door of the house. Sukha—thinking her family would return with food—offered the last cup of rice in the house to the poor beggar. When her family returned home empty-handed and hungry, they discovered her act of impulsive generosity. The husband became enraged and banished her from the household. It seems extreme, but that is how the story goes. This was divorce before the days of alimony. To make matters worse, Sukha was not a young woman when this happened—she was fifty-nine years old. It must have been heartbreaking.

But Sukha picked up the pieces and moved on. She traveled to another region, alone and penniless, and took up life as a beer seller. One of her regular customers was a young woman who came down every day from a nearby mountain to buy a jug of beer. One day, Sukha asked her what she did with the beer she bought.

"I take it to my friend, a hermit named Birwapa who meditates in the remote mountains behind this valley," said the woman.

Sukha felt a wave of spontaneous devotion. Her generous and loving spirit reawakened, and she said, "In that case, take the beer for free!"

The woman took the beer back to Birwapa and recounted to him what had happened. The hermit said to himself, "I should really do something for this woman. I should give her the instructions that lead to enlightenment." Eventually, Sukha met Birwapa. He gave her the instructions, and within a short time she became enlightened. She was sixty-two years old at that time. Who says that age matters on a spiritual path?

Sukha's love was not quenched by circumstances, even dire ones. Even when we feel the least capable of pulling up the warmth of love—love of others, love of life, love of ourselves—even when it feels the farthest from us, it is dormant at worst. When something sparks its reawakening, that may be the moment when a greater kind of love is possible. Sukha did not have to offer free beer to the hermit, but she sensed at some level that the hermit was up to something greater than himself. She intuited his spiritual mission and wanted to contribute to it. In some mysterious way, she must have been ready to develop universal love herself.

So if you ever start to feel like your love is used up, reconsider. Be patient. You will eventually reconnect with the innate seed of love that is inseparable from your wisdom-nature. Once you reconnect, you have a chance to grow more deeply every time you experience love.

Tomorrow, we will look at different ways of loving that increase the joy of loving and reduce the experience of pain. If you widen the scope of love, a relationship that ends in pain is no longer the end of the world. Your relationship to all humanity becomes what sustains you through the darkness and the light.

Day Three

Exercise for Day Three

Forgiving Small Harms

Who has harmed you in a small way in the past, or recently? Think back on the event that made you feel harmed. Are you angry, hurt? What is the feeling like?

Now imagine what you would feel like if you let this go and forgave that person. Feel your body relaxing as you think about it. Notice the difference between holding on and letting go. Can you make a commitment to forgive that person? How does it feel to make such a commitment? If you like, write your promise down.

I promise to forgive _____

for_____

Day Four

Universal Love

To love deeply in one direction makes us more loving in all others.

—Anne-Sophie Swetchine

Today's Date: _____

*I*t is hard to imagine a heart so big that it opens up to include everyone—a love that thinks globally and universally, a love that is boundless, unselfish, and freely given, a love that is honest, true, and unwavering, a love that is unconditional, all-inclusive, and joyous. These are the qualities of a sage's love.

I remember when I was first introduced to the concept of universal love. It was 1985, and I was riding in the back of a beat-up VW Bug on my way to Deer Park, a small Buddhist center nestled in the rolling hills outside of Madison, Wisconsin, to hear my first Tibetan Buddhist teaching. Or maybe not the very first—my childhood included hanging out in zendos and temples of various kinds—but this was the first time I was old enough to grasp the content.

A graduate student was driving and explaining to me the fine points of her dissertation, which turned out to be on the concept of bodhicitta, the Tibetan term for boundless love, unified with perfect wisdom. It sounded like a cool subject to be slaving over. I remember her eyes flitting from the road to the rear-view mirror to see if I was getting what she was explaining to me. I remember she was passionate, taking her hands off the wheel to gesticulate and using the word *archetypal* a lot, like a good grad student should. I probably feigned comprehension. But I was actually kind of blown away. I was thinking, *Who could possibly love like that?* It seemed like too tall an order, too vast a scale. *Everyone* just seemed like too big a group to love. Still, I was intrigued. At the time, I was immersed in a college world where love was a quixotic goal, where physical intimacy was confused with ardor, and where every relationship seemed either vaguely dangerous or impossibly heady, so this new take on love was a breath of fresh air. I was intrigued enough to take out my little notebook and scrawl, *Bodhicitta, universal love? Look up.*

I did look it up. But the references to *bodhicitta* in Buddhist sutras were couched in such flowery rhetoric that the ideal of universal love seemed too divine for an ordinary mortal to aspire to. It was only after years of oral instructions from teachers who practice the methods for developing love that I began to trust that making effort to universalize love is not only worthwhile but can also be profoundly transformative.

Universal love is within reach because it starts with ordinary love. We already have some experience of the qualities of universal love through our relationships with others in our past and now. We have tastes of universal love every single day. One way to see how those tastes can translate into a consistent experience is by reflecting on everyday glimpses of the qualities of universal love. What are these qualities?

Universal love melts boundaries. Generally, when we think about love, there is a sense of how far we are willing to go. Once in a while, there are moments when you surprise yourself and find that a boundary that was once there collapses. For example, like almost everyone, you have probably had the experience of initially meeting someone at a social event and finding their superficial appearance or mannerisms offensive. Then you discover that you really like the person. Without even trying, despite your initial impression, something melts your frozen reactivity. You have witnessed the ability of love to shatter self-imposed limitations. A seeker harnesses that boundary-melting power of love and cultivates it into a spontaneous flow of being, so that reactive defenses are not constructed in the first place.

The Buddha described this boundless quality of a sage's love once when speaking to his monks:

[A monk] lives pervading the whole world with a mind imbued with abundant, exalted, immeasurable loving-kindness, without hostility and without ill will. When the liberation of mind by loving-kindness is developed in this way, no limiting action remains there, none persists there. Just as a vigorous trumpeter could make himself heard without difficulty in all directions, so too, when . . . loving-kindness is developed in this way, no limiting action remains.

When your mind becomes saturated with love, it flows easily into the world, like music. Love accomplishes the liberation of the mind from our own self-imposed fears and aversions. As this liberation occurs, it becomes easier to love with no holds barred.

You can begin to conceive of the power of universal love by working with the boundaries of your own love. Where does your love really begin and end? What kind of boundaries do you put up around yourself? Why? Try to imagine what it would be like if you stretched that boundary a little. What if you moved it out to include more people and living things? Try it.

Universal love evens the terrain. At some level, consciously or subconsciously, most of us label people. Maybe it is our animal survival instinct. We are on the lookout for those who might be dangerous or a threat (destroy them!), those who are of no consequence to us (ignore them!), and those who might become an ally to ensure our success and happiness (court them!). As long as we have attachment, aversion, and apathy, our minds will alternate between perceiving others as friends, enemies, and strangers. This hierarchy of perception sets up a dissonance with a spiritual life-intention, which is to love and care for all.

That is why a seeker must train to even out the ups and downs of perception. How can we even out the terrain? One way is to recollect the contained sphere of a workplace or social group you belong to, where the degree of any one person's partiality becomes more noticeable.

One of my students is a schoolteacher who recently lost her job because she lost control in the classroom.

"What happened?" I asked her on the phone.

"I forgot that the schoolchildren are like my own children," she told me. In her frustration, she lost sight of the schoolteacher's rule to treat each child impartially, as a mother cares for every one of her children. She had started to see one particular child and his friends as the "problem kids" in the classroom. Tension had been building for weeks, and it eventually erupted into an incident that cost my friend her job.

Teachers are required, sometimes by law, to maintain rules of fairness, as are other professionals. This is especially true for those who work with groups or take a leadership role. A police chief is expected to be fair to all the police officers on his staff. A boss is expected to respect all her employees equally. A member of the clergy is expected to care about every person in the congregation.

Consider your own experiences at school and work. These recollections can be helpful for knowing what impartiality feels like, at least in theory. My friend's classroom, like any group bound together in time and place—like the places you live and work—was like a little microcosm of the human family. The problem is, we rarely reach beyond the call of duty, beyond the requirements of our station in life, to develop spiritual equanimity.

Spiritual equanimity is more challenging than professional impartiality. Spiritual equanimity is more than the attitude of "I will tolerate you, if you tolerate me." A sage injects what he or she already knows of impartiality with love, a feeling that is warm, accepting, and forgiving. A sage does not stop with neutrality, but moves forward into an attitude that is affectionate and inviting. Patrul Rinpoche, a great cave yogi of Tibet, said:

> The image given for truly boundless equanimity is a banquet given by a sage. When the great sages of old offered feasts, they would invite everyone, high or low, powerful or weak, good or bad, exceptional or ordinary, without making any distinction whatsoever. Likewise, our attitude toward all beings throughout space should be a vast feeling of

compassion, encompassing them all equally. Train your mind until you reach such a state of boundless equanimity.

Universal love does not exclude anyone and goes out equally to everyone. So at the table of your love, do not make a place setting for some people and neglect to invite others. Instead, train to be more and more inclusive and forgiving, evening out the terrain of your tendency to pull some people close and hold others at a distance. How can you train this way in the social microcosms of your life?

Universal love tears up contracts. One of my favorite stories about the unconditional nature of a sage's love comes from the biography of Yeshe Tsogyal. Once when Yeshe Tsogyal was traveling from Tibet to Nepal, she was stalked by seven thieves. At that time, travelers did most of their bartering in gold dust, so the thieves were hoping this pilgrim might be carrying some. And indeed she was. But instead of fleeing or resisting the advances of the thieves, the spiritual heroine turned to face them. Envisioning them as buddhas, she beautifully arranged everything she was carrying and offered it to them while singing a song to go along with the gift. They were so surprised and touched by her gesture of complete trust and love that they lost their aggression and dropped their plan to rob her.

It seems as if such a situation would call for fear or aggression, not love. The role of the thief is to threaten, and the role of the victim is to be afraid or fight back. But Yeshe Tsogyal had trained not to put much stock in roles or to place provisions on her love. She did not have the idea, "I will love someone *if* that person is not a bandit. I will provide someone with whatever they need *if* they do not rob me." Paying attention to social conventions was not her practice; loving no matter what was her practice.

How might you tear up implicit contracts and disregard the roles of social conventions in favor of loving completely? How can you work on the practice of loving more unconditionally? Of course, you should try to keep relationship contracts, such as marriage vows, clergy vows, or parental responsibilities. But the love itself is not a contract, and therefore it cannot be contravened.

Exercise for Day Four

Assessing Boundaries

Consider: What kind of boundaries do you place around your feelings? Are there people whom you do not love because of what they do or have done? What kind of "ifs" do you put on love? Now consider, is it possible to love someone with no "ifs"? Consider whether it is possible to love without agreeing with or condoning another's actions. Are there any valid reasons to withhold love?

Now think of one person from whom you withhold the feeling of love, not entirely but somewhat. Can you imagine what it would be like to push your boundary out with this person and let yourself feel a love with fewer conditions, at least sometimes? Visualize for yourself what this would be like. What do you gain by withholding love? What do you lose by giving it?

Day Five

No Ifs, No Buts, No Self

I will tell you a deep secret. Pay attention! All faults are your own. All good qualities belong to others. The point: give victory to others, and take defeat for yourself. There is nothing else to know.

—Langri Tangpa

Today's Date: _____

*Y*esterday, we considered that universal love has no "ifs." Okay, so it may not have "ifs," but might it not have "buts"?

Universal love is nonjudgmental. There are no *buts* in universal love. Can we not all relate to the irony of the guy seeing a therapist who says, "I love her unconditionally, but . . . "? To the extent that you add a *but* to your love, you move further away from thinking like a sage. The *but* is indicative of your preoccupation with a superficial and transitory trait—that annoying habit she has of leaving dirty cups in the sink, the shortness of his temper, the way she never seems to stop talking. In the big picture, such traits do not matter as much as wisdom-nature matters. A trait does not define a person. It does not express that person's deepest being.

As uncomfortable as it might sound, we might not even be witnessing a fault. We might be witnessing our own fault-finding attitude. One of the great things about many teachers of the Tibetan tradition is that they have a way of not sugarcoating that possibility. Mochokpa, a great twelfth-century cave meditator of Tibet, sings in one of his songs:

Day Five

The extent to which you deal with your own mind—and not that of
others—is the extent to which self-centeredness decreases.

Put another way, working with and training your own mind is the
path to selflessness and empathy. Analyzing and judging the minds of
others is the path to self-centeredness. Nonjudgmental love is developed right in the frontier of your own mind. So put energy into observing your own faults—whatever impedes the progress of selfless love—
not the faults of others.

Not judging does not mean that you cannot find fault with someone
else's actions, but finding fault with peoples' actions does not mean you
have to find fault with the people themselves. If you can really take this
practice to heart, you will begin to view your own faults differently. Like
the faults of others, they are not your deepest self. They do not express
your most authentic being. As you become more tolerant of others, you
become more tolerant of yourself. With that comes an ability to both
recognize and be patient with your own mistakes.

Universal love is selfless. Selfless love does not love with a motive. It is
love that loses itself in the act of loving. The great Indian master Asanga,
perhaps the earliest and most revered spokesperson for the nature of
universal love, said:

> When she attains the attitude of the equality of self and others or of
> caring for others more than for herself, then she feels that others' aims
> outweigh her own. What then is individualism? And what is altruism?

A sage in the act of loving is so focused on serving the aims of others that
she loses the sense of a barrier between self and other. For such a person,
at that moment of selfless love, even the concepts of individualism or
altruism lose their meaning. How can there be individualism without
a self? How can there be altruism without a giver and receiver? A sage
dissolves the dualism in love and uses it as a path to selflessness.

Do we have moments of selfless love? I think everyone does. Even animals. During a three-year silent retreat, I discovered a litter of kittens in the woodshed behind the retreat house. They were nestled in the box where we stored kindling. The next day, I went out to check on them. The light was dim in the woodshed, so I leaned over and reached into the box to feel around for the kittens. To my dismay, I heard a growl. I pulled my hand back just in time to avoid being swiped by the mother. I opened the door behind me to get a better look. There she was, backed up against the litter, the hair standing straight up on her back, hissing and growling. I thought, *Surely if I get up close, she will get scared and run*. I put on a glove and approached her again. I reached out my hand until it was a foot away from her. She had absolutely no intention of budging. Instead, she growled more loudly, bared her fangs and hissed with an expression of absolute ferocity. She swiped again.

Here I was, perhaps fifteen times her weight, and she was ready to fight me to the death! Never mind that she could never be a match for so large a predator, if I were one. I was truly impressed, not by her fury, but by the instinct behind it. You might say it was mere terror, but she could easily have escaped the situation. For that mother cat (who eventually became our pet Pema), her life was less important to her than the lives of her offspring. She did not even have to think about it for a split second. Abandonment was not an option. She just leaped into a mode of ferocious protectiveness. It really made me think. What if I could develop a love that powerful, assured, selfless, and energetic for every living thing?

Universal love is compassionate. Compassionate love is a love that feels *with* others. A sage does not block out the world's pain but takes the higher road of empathy. As Asanga put it:

> The compassionate genius understands that everything included in
> the life-cycle is naturally suffering. . . . When she observes the natural
> suffering of the world, the loving [bodhisattva] suffers; yet she knows

just what it is as well as the means to avoid it, and so she does not become exhausted.

Pain and suffering are an inevitable part of life, of the endless cycle of death and rebirth (or birth and death if you prefer). It is not hard for us to observe this in our everyday experience. How many hours can any one of us go through in a day without experiencing some kind of uneasiness, irritation, physical pain, or mental discomfort? How long can any one of us go without witnessing the pain of someone else?

How often do we seek to escape from pain—take a painkiller, shove the unpleasant news story out of the mind, ignore the beggar, avoid visiting a dying friend? When we see someone else in pain, we naturally empathize, but we feel helpless. Thinking there is nothing that can be done, we freeze up or exit the situation. Sages are also not numb to suffering. They feel the pain of the world but are not paralyzed or exhausted by it. Why? Because a sage has the wisdom to hold the big picture. A sage knows the person suffering is a sage-in-the-making, and that the moment of suffering is just a temporary blip on the great arc of this person's spiritual journey.

In the presence of suffering, a lot can be done. Our tendency is to avoid being a witness to suffering. We want to run and hide from it. Instead of walking away, use your contact with suffering as an opportunity to identify with the pain of others. Put that identification into action on behalf of the person suffering—who is at that moment embodying the suffering of all humanity. Enlightenment would not be possible without the presence of suffering. Asanga:

> If [a spiritual] genius could not bear up under suffering, she would have no ambition for the sake of beings.

If you do not develop a tenderness of heart at the root of your spiritual practice, you will not be able to do whatever is necessary to serve others. Witnessing, knowing, and accepting your own suffering and the world's suffering fuels the ambition to continue on the long odyssey to communal awakening.

Universal love is joyous. Even though a sage empathizes with the world's suffering, he is not depressed. Why? If you fully accept the presence of suffering, and even embrace discomfort as a path to awakening love, you stop fighting against suffering. What would happen if you stopped resisting your own suffering and the suffering of others?

My husband is a nurse working on a postsurgical unit in a hospital in Boston. Naturally, on a postsurgical unit, pain management is in effect for every patient. There is a lot of pain after surgery. In his first year working as a health-care professional, he observed that there were two kinds of patients: those who accepted their illness and those who fought it. Those who accepted their general state of debilitation coped well with pain. Those who did not accept their illness coped poorly with pain. I asked him if he had a theory about that.

He replied, "Patients who accept their illness do not build on top of their physical pain with mental suffering. The patients who do not accept their illness are intolerant of the fact that they are in the hospital and are usually miserable. They even say things like, 'Why me?' and 'I want to go home right now!' and 'This should not be happening to me.' Some of them even get up and try to leave, chest-tube and all! It is as if every ounce of their energy resists the reality that they see with their eyes. These patients suffer at least twice as much as the other patients, who can be cheerful, joking, and good natured even when in a lot of physical pain. They seem to understand that it will all be over in a few days, as their surgical wound heals."

The Buddha taught that empathetic suffering is like the physical suffering of a good-natured patient. Just as a good-natured patient meets his own pain with tolerance and compassion, it is possible for us to witness and feel the pain of others with tolerance and compassion. Empathetic pain is like water on the flower of universal love, so with practice, it might even be possible eventually to meet this pain with joy.

Day Five

How can it be that we would be glad to be moved by another person's suffering? When we are happy and comfortable, do we not want to stay that way? When we are in our comfort zone, the thought of feeling the suffering of others sounds scary. We imagine our heart might break open if we bear witness to the sufferings of others. But this fear is largely unfounded. Our heart will not really break open. Our world will not implode. Instead, we will begin to understand imaginatively what it means to be that person, and we will thus come to know another's pain intimately. This is the beginning of real compassion, a compassion that connects us to the human family in a way no other emotion can. Suffering is not a threat; it is a fact of the human condition, and our acceptance of that fact is the beginning of compassion.

Exercise for Day Five

Overcoming the Judging Mind

Consider: In what ways does judgment get in the way of loving those closest to you? Is your love clouded with judgment?

One remedy for judging others is to discern and be honest with yourself about your own shortcomings. What shortcomings do you have? Take some time to reflect on this, and make a small mental list. What if you took the energy you used to dwell on the actions of others and used it instead to pay attention to and work on your own shortcomings? What is worse, the tendency to find fault in others or the faults you judge others to have?

Day Six

Four Ways of Perceiving Others

Each one of them is Jesus in disguise.
—Mother Teresa

Today's Date: _____

*H*ow you love is greatly influenced by how you perceive others. If you perceive someone as a friend, you will feel differently around that person than if you were to approach her as an enemy. If you approach someone with suspicion, you will feel differently in his presence than if you were to approach him with trust. When you approach someone, what kind of attitude do you bring with you? To deepen love, a sage starts by seeing the people right around her as intimately connected to the human family. In that way, every single interaction contains the world and becomes a challenge for developing and widening the scope of love to include more and more people.

Every person is your only child. Joe works in a supermarket chain at a checkout stand. Every day, he sees hundreds of people pass before him. After awhile, he just begins to tune out the people who come into his line. He does not look in their eyes or smile. He just wants to get through the day so that he can get home and relax and be away from people. Almost every time I go shopping, I see someone like this at the checkout stand, and I think, *That reminds me of me!*

The people we pass on the street, stand beside on the subway, and squeeze fruit next to in the supermarket are strangers. We meet them with an indifference that we excuse with the thought, *I do not know this person. He is a stranger*. But what is stranger—that person or the attitude with which we meet him or her? Strange that we miss the chance to make connection with this member of our human family. Strange that the concept *stranger* has a stronger hold over us than the recollection that this is someone's beloved child, mother, or father. How can we change our daily interactions?

Most of us have heard the saying, "Every parent's child is the most beautiful child in the world." The parent-child relationship is often used as a metaphor for how we can relate to others. A mother's or father's love for a child can be extraordinarily powerful. A parent will sacrifice anything for the child, and the sacrifice is made with genuine love and affection. A parent's love comes naturally, because he or she really does want the best for the child. A parent is also extremely forgiving of a child and looks beyond the child's faults to see the good qualities and potentials within.

If all humanity were your children, how would you perceive others: your neighbor, your grocer, your financial consultant, your prison guard, your roommate? The sage looks on each and every being as an only child. As the Buddha put it:

> From the marrow of their bones,
> Bodhisattvas view every living being as their only child.
> In this way, they consistently have the desire to benefit others.

So when you see someone approaching, try to think of them as your own blood, a member of your family. Work with your habitual reactions to having the person in your presence. How could you feel disturbed by the presence of your only child, the dearest person in the world to you? How could you be jealous? How could you feel competitive with him or her? Keep in mind the person's inner beauty as a mother would for her child. See what happens!

Every person is your parent. You are the recipient of immeasurable kindness from your parents. They gave you a flesh-and-blood body. They fed and clothed you when you were helpless to take care of yourself. When you were sick, they nursed you. When you needed comfort, they cared about you. There is no way we can repay them. No matter how complicated your relationship with your parents might be, you are forever in their debt.

How would it be if you related to each person with the understanding that you were forever in his or her debt? You would treat the person with respect and gratitude, as if because of that person you are alive now. And that is not really so far from the truth. Even if that person is not a parent, he or she has been kind to someone. Because of that person, someone may be alive who would not have been otherwise. Does it matter if it was not you personally?

Furthermore, you have good reason to seek out and appreciate the goodness of others as if they were your parents. Why? Remembering kindness is one of the deep roots of developing love. As Gampopa put it, "Developing [love] depends on appreciating the kindness of every living being." And the Dalai Lama echoes this: "The roots of all goodness lie in the soil of appreciation for goodness." So to fertilize that soil, work with appreciating the goodness of everyone around you.

If you have a loving relationship with one or both of your parents, the parent-perception is a good perception to try out. I was lucky to have a close and loving connection to both my parents, so this is a perception I use a lot. When you find yourself in the field of vision or interaction with someone, try saying to yourself, *This is my mother (or father), in essence*. As you interact, even if it is just with your eyes, try to interact with that person with the same love and trust that you have for a parent. Think about the kindnesses your parents showed you and transfer the gratefulness you feel for your parents to him or her.

Every person is your best friend. When you approach a friend, you feel like a friend. You start with a basis of trust and basic liking or love. When a friend needs help or is in trouble, you come immediately to give her a hand. What would your life be like if you began approaching strangers (in safe situations) as if you were best friends? In Buddhist sources, sages are sometimes called "the friends of the world." Try approaching someone, especially someone you do not know, or someone you do not like very much, with this perception. Shantideva, the great Indian Buddhist master, recommended:

> One who has become self-controlled should always have a smiling face.
> Give up frowning and grimacing, be the first to greet and be a friend to
> the world.

So when someone approaches, be a friend to him, even before you speak. Try to release your fear, anxiety, nervousness, aversion, and irritation. If you have previous experience with this person, forget your history and start over. If you do not know the person at all, start with the basis of a friend's trust.

Shantideva also said:

> You should always look straight at people, as if drinking them in with
> the eyes, thinking, "Relying on you alone, I will awaken."

We will not awaken—that is, reach our full potential—without help. It is only through the path of learning to love others unconditionally that we will fulfill the spiritual journey. Therefore, every person—whoever approaches us—is our best friend and helper. Keeping this in mind, do not seek to avoid people. Direct your eyes straight at the person in your field of interaction, and extend your friendship to him or her openly. This person, the one in your presence right now, is your best friend on the spiritual path! Cultivating this kind of attitude can do wonders for how we relate to people.

Everyone is a sage. In the "Song of Zazen," Zen master Hakuin Zenji says:

> All beings are by nature Buddha,
> as ice by nature is water.
> Apart from water there is no ice;
> apart from beings, no Buddha.

There is no way to talk about awakening without including each and every person in that equation. Buddha, the archetypal sage, lives because of beings. No matter what form people take, they are still buddha-like by virtue of their inherent purity. People bring Buddha into the world. That includes you and everyone else. But it can be a challenge to maintain that understanding in all social situations. Perhaps an easier, or alternative, perception to maintain is that every person has much more in common with you than they have disparity with you. If you look at your most fundamental hopes, you can see the hopes of every person reflected there. If you look at your deepest fears, you can see the fears of every person there. Other than the object of your hopes and fears, what is the real difference? Just like you, she—the imagined person across from you—wishes for happiness. Just like you, she wishes to avoid suffering.

Try approaching another while mentally repeating the phrase, *Just like me*. This simple technique will help you see past that person's appearance and her gender or race or religion or background. Even if she has different values from yours, votes differently, is on a different path and has a very different personality, you will begin to relate to her on a fundamental ground of sameness. Even if you have a history with her, you can rewrite that history starting today. Therefore, the next time someone comes into your field of vision or interaction, think about the human qualities that essentially bond you. Mentally repeat, *This person is just like me.*

Experiment with these four ways of perceiving others—as your child, parent, best friend, or a sage—and see what feels good to you. I use all of them myself. You may find that different ones help your relationships in different ways. Some are more effective than others on certain occasions or with certain people. Try out one of these four ways today as an exercise. Choose someone at work, a family member, or a stranger. If you are brave and apply these ways all week, you will begin to see a change in your relationships. Use them especially with people with whom you have an "issue" or at times when you feel challenged.

These ways of perceiving are effective even with people you do not know very well, such as your grocer or someone on the street. Such people are a good place to start, because when working with a stranger, we are sometimes less afraid. We do not worry about how our beginning attempts at using these tools might reflect on us. At first, it is a challenge to work with the four ways. But consider the alternative, which is to continue with old patterns of thought and behavior. With skill, and through trial and error, you will find ways to work with them that benefit your mind and relationships.

Exercise for Day Six

Approaching Others Anew

Again, here are the four ways of perceiving others:

- Every person is your child.
- Every person is your parent.
- Every person is your best friend.
- Every person is a sage.

When someone is moving into your field of interaction, pick one of the four ways to perceive them. Like a mantra, say to yourself, *My friend!* or *My only child!* or *My mother!* or *Just like me!*

Proceed to interact, keeping the thought in mind of your new relationship to this person.

Day Seven

Growing Love through Contemplation

To love is to admire with the heart. To admire is to love with the mind.

—Théophile Gautier

Today's Date: _____

When you are on a spiritual journey, you are moving in the direction of trusting that your potential for goodness can go further than you thought possible. You are starting to understand that the only thing keeping you from loving big is your belief that you cannot. Confidence that you can develop a greater scope of love grows as you begin to push the boundaries of your love using approaches such as the four ways of perceiving others. Taking this step requires a bit of courage and a willingness to take small risks.

Another approach to pushing the boundaries is through contemplation. This week's contemplation is focused on helping you awaken love, tapping into the ocean that is locked deep in your heart right now.

This contemplation begins with thinking of someone you love. It might be the person to whom you feel closest. It might be a spouse, a parent, a friend, or a pet. It can be one of your benefactors from Day Two. It does not even have to be anyone you really love, if you cannot think of someone. It can just be someone you like a lot. It can be someone you feel friendly toward. Visualize that person in front of you. A visualization is a mental picture or image that you create in your mind, in the same way that you see a dream image. If you are new to visualization, it can help to have a picture of the person or pet in front of you. Do not worry if you cannot envision the person vividly. It suffices if you have the feeling that they are in front of you.

Imagine the person is in the room with you. How do you feel in his or her presence? Conjure up the good feeling you have when you are around this friend. Recreate the warmest feelings you have with him or her. Think back to when you had a happy time around this person and let yourself feel that way again, right in the meditation session.

Now imagine that the feeling takes a *form*. It is a warm, glowing light in your heart. It grows as you gaze upon the imagined friend in front of you. As it grows, it spreads out so that it fills your whole chest area. Let it grow until you feel like you cannot possibly contain it any longer.

Then let the warm light go out of your body through your nostrils with every exhalation. It flows out to your friend and touches him or her. Your friend is pleased to feel your love so viscerally. Allow the love to pass through your friend's body and radiate farther with every exhalation.

The love-light spreads out with every exhalation to permeate the world. Imagine it touching and filling the bodies of everyone in its path. They receive the love viscerally, like a gift. They are filled with warmth, comfort, gratitude, and happiness.

At the end of visualizations in the Buddhist tradition, there is a phase called the *dissolution*. In that phase, the things you have been visualizing dissolve. In this case, imagine that the person in front of you dissolves into light. Then imagine the entire world around you dissolves into light. Now imagine there is nothing at all except love and light; not even a "you" exists.

Rest calmly and peacefully in the feeling of love and in the afterglow of the deed of loving.

Say your Dedication Prayer at the end of the session.

This visualization to awaken love is a powerful tool for appreciating that your love can grow and that you are capable of stimulating love at will. Like anything else, love is a habit pattern and a thought pattern. The more you love, the easier it becomes. But it is important not to cling to this visualization exercise too literally. You should not dwell on whether you are engaging in a psychic exercise that has real results. The main thing is that you are training your mind and heart to love so that

Dharma Tip

When you first do a meditation or contemplation, you may find yourself needing to refer to the instructions often in order to remember what to do. You can open your eyes to read each step, then close them again and do that step. It is like following a recipe or reading a piece of music for the first time. If you keep this practice up, after awhile you will not need to look at the instructions; you will have them memorized. (Also see "Resources for Further Exploration" at the back of this book, which includes information about downloading audio files of instructions for these meditations from the Web.)

you can move on to the next part of your journey: bringing the sage in you into the world through activity.

Exercise for Day Seven

Contemplation to Awaken a Sage's Love

- The Three Arrivals: Arrive with body, breath, and mind.
- Say your Awakening Prayer aloud.
- Relax and breathe.
- Imagine a person you love in front of you.
- While focusing on that person, allow the feeling of love to grow and take the form of a warm light in your chest area.
- Let it grow until it overflows with each exhalation, radiating out to the person and suffusing his or her body.
- After awhile, let the love flow beyond the person into the world. Allow your love to radiate as far as it will go, permeating the bodies of everyone in its path.

Day Seven

- At the end of the session, imagine that the person before you dissolves, the world dissolves, and there is only love.
- At the end of the session, dedicate your contemplation, using your Dedication Praycr.

May I know myself to be worthy of love.
May I recognize every being as my parent, my only child,
my best friend, a sage.
May I learn to love like a sage: universally, boundlessly,
impartially, and unconditionally.

Action expresses priorities.

—Gandhi

Week Five

Be Magnanimous

Step five is to cultivate magnanimous deeds. This week you will discover how acting enlightened makes you feel more enlightened.

What does it mean to be *magnanimous?* The word literally means "greatness of soul" or "high-mindedness." I like the word because it carries with it the notion of *size.* Someone who is magnanimous is someone with a spacious mind and a big heart, someone who forgives easily and laughs easily. This may not be a frame of mind with which we can always identify. But who says you have to *be* big hearted to *act* big hearted?

Day One

Begin with Action

Every act counts. Every thought and emotion counts, too. This is all the path we have.

—Pema Chodron

Today's Date: _____

At least half of you is what you do. The other half is what you think and feel. By doing, you become who you will be tomorrow. The Buddha put it this way:

If you want to know where you have been in the past, look at your mind now. If you want to know where you are going in the future, look at your *actions* now.

Who you are now, with all your habits, emotions, and thoughts, is the result of what you have done in the past. What you are doing right now, in the present, is creating and shaping your future reality, and it is also shaping your mind. What you do really matters.

This is an empowering thought. It means that you do not have to "get yourself together" before acting like a compassionate sage. Your outer actions and inner cultivation of your wisdom-nature are interdependent. Why not work on them simultaneously? Why not become a sage inside and in the world at the same time? Instead of thinking by leaps, you can think in small steps, pondering: *What will I do* today *to take a small step toward putting my aspirations and intentions into action? How will I put love into action* today?

No action is too small or insignificant to shape you and your future. Small steps can be big.

Week Five

I remember 1988 as one of the pivotal years of my life. It was the year I took nun's vows and decided to take on the Buddhist path with full intensity. I spent the year's beginning with my teacher Kalu Rinpoche in Bodh Gaya, India, where the Buddha is said to have first become enlightened 2,500 years ago. At the time, Kalu Rinpoche was a wizened old man who looked and even sounded quite a bit like Yoda. (A rumor circulated for a while among Buddhists that the Yoda character was modeled on Kalu Rinpoche—and it may be true.)

Bodh Gaya is a pilgrimage spot for Buddhists, who gather there to say prayers and make aspirations under the bodhi tree, a huge, ancient, big-leafed tree that is said to have descended from the very tree under which the Buddha meditated. Kalu Rinpoche invited us all there to accompany him in reciting aspiration prayers for a month.

The first morning I was very excited at the thought of spending all morning in prayer with him and his monks under the tree. We settled under the great umbrella of leaves as the sun rose, and we began to pray. There were all kinds of animals in the park around us . . . especially dogs and birds. The chanting of the monks rose up in a deep and soothing melody. As soon as the chanting was underway, I noticed Kalu Rinpoche motion to one of his monks, who brought him some food. I wondered if maybe he had not eaten breakfast. But then, as we all chanted, Rinpoche began breaking up the bread and tossing it to all the dogs and birds within reach. He even crumbled up tiny pieces for the insects near his seat. Pretty soon, all the dogs in the vicinity of the tree were there, and perhaps all the birds and insects too. As they came, I noticed Rinpoche leaning over in his seat, his face alight with the most loving and gentle smile, as if he were talking to them.

"What is he doing?" I asked one of the monks.

"He is reciting prayers for them. He wants them to hear. Even if they do not understand, it makes a connection with them. He always does that . . . you will see."

And indeed, every morning for that month, Rinpoche fed all the animals while he prayed. The chanting was mixed with barks and twitters as more and more creatures joined us under the tree. He saw an opportunity to do something beneficial for some living creatures within his reach, and he just did it. His small act of including even the little animals and insects in his prayer sessions touched me more deeply than any of the many meditation instructions we received from him that month.

Rinpoche showed us that month in Bodh Gaya that actions do not need to be big to be significant. If your intention is big and inclusive, if your heart is magnanimous, small actions take on a whole new meaning. While Rinpoche made aspirations with his speech to humanity and all living creatures, big and small, he made the aspirations real with his hands. He moved his commitment to serve humanity and all living things into action whenever he saw a chance.

Exercise for Day One

Observe Your Actions

Three or four times today, check in with your actions. What are you doing at this moment? Consider: *When I look at the state of my body and mind now, what does that say about my past and where my energy has been channeled? When I look at my actions now, what kind of future am I creating through this action in which I am engaged? In other words, what kind of karma am I creating?*

Day Two

The Power of Shifting the Center

When the mind turns to others, it is engaging in something that is extraordinary. What it is about to do is amazing. It is going to step outside, away from itself, and be less self-concerned. It is going to look at the concerns of others in the world.

—Sakyong Mipham Rinpoche

Today's Date: _____

How do we know if our actions measure up to the status of a sage's actions or are moving in that direction? Is there a quick yardstick for what sets wise actions apart? Yes. A sage's actions are *other-centered* actions. Usually our actions are self-serving, because our attention is directed toward our personal goals and wishes. We are principally concerned with manipulating things "out there" so that we maximize our own profit, ensure our survival, and acquire the things, experiences, and circumstances that we believe will bring us happiness and comfort. We are self-centered; our actions are motivated by our own interests and aims, with an eye on our own happiness. We rarely act from a space that is principally concerned with the good of others and with their welfare and comfort.

You can begin to cultivate a magnanimous heart by shifting the balance of your actions. Other-centered actions are whatever actions follow from shifting your focus from yourself to others. "Others" is not just an amorphous, anonymous group. It is whomever comes to mind, and particularly—at first—whomever you have contact with in your life. Shifting your focus from your own concerns to the concerns of others is not as difficult as it might sound. It just takes a little reflection and imagination.

Take an ordinary example. Suppose you are loading your car with groceries in a supermarket parking lot, and you notice an elderly woman having trouble opening the trunk of her car. If you are in a hurry, you might ignore her. Or, if you are not, you might go over to see if you can assist her. If you go over to assist her, you might do so for two reasons. One is that you remember your mother's voice saying, *"Honey, you should always help out an old person on the street."* The other reason is that some part of you thought, *What if I were she?* You put yourself in her place and empathized on that basis.

An other-centered attitude is one in which the person thinks, *What if I were in her place?* That person imaginatively takes the other's place and feels *with* him or her. This kind of other-centered thinking and feeling is much more powerful than simply acting in what we perceive as an ethical manner because someone told us to. Why? Because it takes our experience of our own personal wants and needs and turns it to our advantage. Whatever it is that you like and want from life—your deepest wish to be happy—is what others like and want, too. If your commitment is to serve humanity, in whatever ways you have chosen, you must care about the needs, hopes, and dreams of others. You must care about their happiness as if it were your own. This is accomplished by not merely seeing their needs, hopes, and dreams, but by *feeling* their needs, hopes, and dreams with them.

When I first moved into the monastery at the age of twenty-one, I remember thinking about the abbot, *If I were drowning in an ocean, he is the person I would want on the beach.* He was poised—seemingly at all times—to spring into action in ways that were startling to my novice Buddhist eyes. He was the abbot! How could he always be jumping up to help someone carry a bag, going to the drugstore for a nun who needed medicine, holding a blowtorch for Tom, the monastery handyman, or stirring the soup for the cook? It seemed incongruous. At the time, I thought this was just a personality trait, but as I became more acquainted with him and people like him, I began to understand that it had to do with a general attitude of persons training to be spiritual sages. He had a *magnanimous heart,* one that embraced everyone and was

167

open to their concerns. The scope of his magnanimity came from daily reinforcement, through prayer and recollection, of his commitment to his quest to serve every single living being. Shantideva, author of the essential Buddhist classic *The Bodhisattva's Way of Life*, could have been describing this lama when he said:

> One should do nothing other than benefit living beings, either directly
> or indirectly; and for the sake of living beings alone, subordinate every-
> thing to their collective awakening.

Serving others is the sage's purpose. Therefore, to cultivate magnanimous actions, start by looking outward for ways to serve those around you.

Exercise for Day Two

Shift the Center

Today, take note when you are irritated with someone else. It happens to us all, sometimes just mildly, every day. When you encounter this situation, ask yourself, *How does the person with whom I am now irritated experience this moment?* Try to put yourself in the other person's shoes and put your own irritation aside temporarily. Imagine: How does it really feel to be this person right now? What is he or she thinking and feeling?

Day Three

Give It and Get It

Sometimes your joy is the source of your smile, but sometimes your smile can be the source of your joy.

—Thich Nhat Hanh

Today's Date: _____

*I*n the Buddhist context, generosity—the attitude and actions of giving—is the very first quality a seeker on the path works to perfect. Why is giving, over all other relative qualities, so important? Because giving is the epitome of other-centered action. It is magnanimity given hands and feet. When you give, it is possible to have a self-centered motivation. But because all acts of giving involve some degree of shifting the center from self to other, there is less self-centeredness involved than if you refrain from giving. This is especially true when sacrifice is involved, when you give up a little in your giving.

Sacrifice implies both exchange and purpose. When you make a sacrifice, you give away something in exchange for an outcome. For example, you give up some of your free time to help your son with his homework so that he might succeed in school and later in his chosen career. On one hand, you are temporarily inconvenienced by this gift of your time, since you might have other things crowding your to-do list on a given day. On the other hand, you recognize that the exchange has a positive outcome. Your son will succeed in school, and his life will be better for it.

With regard to the exchange aspect of sacrifice, it usually plays out in one of two ways: as an ambivalent sacrifice or as an empathetic one. In the first scenario, your son asks you for help with his homework, and you say, "Okay." You sit down with your son (let us say his name is Blake)

169

and look through his math book with him. But inside, you are thinking about the Red Sox game. Inside you are fretting about whether someone is going to hit a home run and you might miss it. You help Blake with his homework, but you are not really happy about it. It feels like a burden. You do it, but you are not fully into it, not fully willing. You make an ambivalent sacrifice.

Another way it could go is that Blake asks you for help. You still say, "Okay." You sit down with Blake and turn your attention to him. What is it like to be Blake right now? How is he looking at this? Who am I to him? When you consider these questions, you take an empathetic stance, and it is easier to enter the activity wholeheartedly. Blake is your access to humanity at this very moment. To turn away from him when he needs you is to turn away from humanity. At this moment, you are Blake's sage. With that thought in mind, it becomes easier to step up to the plate and give your time attentively, lovingly, and joyously.

You forget about the Red Sox for now—watching the game is not nearly as pertinent to your life's intention as an act of giving. Empathetic sacrifice is a natural outcome of shifting the center. The moment you turn your attention to Blake's imagined internal world, you are simultaneously him and yourself, and this shift *makes you forget that you are giving up anything*. When you enter into that mode, you dissolve a boundary between the recipient and the giver. The difference between ambivalent sacrifice and empathetic sacrifice has to do with attitude. In the latter case, you take joy in permeable boundaries.

I like to think of these small daily sacrifices as *magnanimous deeds*. You probably have no trouble seeing yourself as a doer of acts, but a doer of deeds? That takes a little more thought. To be a doer of deeds, you need to have your eye on the *how* and the *why* of your actions. A deed is an action in which the how and why are front and center. Magnanimous deeds are actions in which the how and why are joined with a magnanimous heart, a heart that is open, loving, generous, selfless, and kind.

Now, at first it may seem a stretch to imagine you could become a magnanimous doer of deeds this week. But that can easily happen. And this is why: all you have to do to become a doer of deeds is simply to do something other-centered with intention. This especially means doing things that take you a little out of your comfort zone. Your comfort zone, after all, is the little picture. Your spiritual journey is the big picture. When you do something generous with intention, with the big picture in mind, you move into the space of deeds.

If doing a deed stopped with the action, that would be one thing. But the doing of deeds changes you. You cannot give without giving up a little of your center. And when you give up your center, you slip into magnanimous territory. This takes some effort, but you have to start with making some effort at generosity before generosity becomes effortless. If someone approaches and you are happy to see her, you might smile naturally because you feel happy—that generosity takes little effort. But imagine that a coworker of whom you are not particularly fond approaches you. At that moment, you are tempted to put on your *Do not bother me* face or your *You again!* face. You will tend to refrain from being generous with this person in any way. What if instead you said to yourself, *I think I will be generous and give her a smile, even though I do not feel like smiling. Just like me, she has a wisdom-nature.* And you make the extra effort to flash her a smile. Something will happen to you. You might actually feel a little happier. You might feel a little more open to her. You might feel a little more generous. You have just taken action as your path to magnanimity. When you give in this way, you get it.

Becoming magnanimous is a luxuriously long process. Growing a heart that is open, loving, generous, selfless, and kind takes time. Every opportunity to give that you notice this week is a step in that direction. And the most profound ways to give are often the most overlooked. Most ways of giving cost us nothing but getting over the initial fear of letting go of our self-center.

Exercise for Day Three

Give Physically—the Gift of Smiling

Today, try a "smiling experiment." Every day, we pass people on the street, interact with them over a counter, pass by their desks, without giving them our full attention. Today, make a conscious effort to smile at some of these people, at least three of them. When you smile at them, join the smile with an inner wish for their well-being. After you try this, consider these three questions: (1) How did the person respond to your smile? (2) Did smiling change the tone of your interaction with that person? (3) How did you feel internally after this interaction? Did smiling change your state of mind?

Day Four

Many Ways to Give

We can do no great things, only small things with great love.
—Mother Teresa

Today's Date: _____

There are many ways to be generous, and some of the most profound gifts are not things. To give, no particular external conditions are necessary: you do not have to be wealthy. To give, no particular internal conditions are necessary: You do not have to feel like a saint. You do not even have to think of yourself as a generous person. All you need is a little creativity and a little willingness to try out some new ways of acting. To be a doer of magnanimous deeds begins with identifying some ways to express magnanimity in action. Opportunities abound; where there are living beings, there is a field for generosity. So when someone comes into your field of interaction, begin by asking the question, How can I be magnanimous with this person?

Material giving. Material giving loosens the grip that the material world holds on us, and it is a good remedy for the tendency to cling to things as "mine." If you are on a spiritual journey, the word *mine* loses some of its force, edged out by the word *ours*. If you are fully committed to your life-intention, to the mission to serve others, what is "yours" really is not yours alone. If your purpose in life is to serve, then everything you own belongs as much to those you serve as it does to you. How can you have entitlement to something that you do not really own? You are the temporary overseer, a caretaker, of that property. Therefore, when you give something material away, you are not really losing or giving up anything. You are just sharing it with its mutual owners, with the human family to which we all belong.

Material giving helps us cut through attachment.

Our tendency to get attached to things in the material world is strong. That very attachment is the cause of our suffering. It is the mind of attachment that worries about losing what it has, that suffers when something is lost, that pines for what it does not yet have. The mind of attachment is a discontented mind. Material giving, even in cases where we resist it or it is hard to do, compels us to let go of that attachment to some extent. Even if we continue to cling to what is given, we are forced into a situation where we have to face our attachment.

But material giving is also important for other reasons. For one, it expresses your life-intention in concrete action. To be truly free, we are ultimately going to have to give up selfishness, meaning we are going to have to give up and let go of everything for the sake of those we serve. As Shantideva put it:

> Surrendering everything is nirvana, and my mind seeks nirvana. Since I must surrender everything eventually, it is better that I give it to living beings now.

If we are eventually going to have to fully devote our time, energy, and resources to helping others, why wait? You are probably not ready to surrender everything, but just having the mind that looks ahead to where you are aspiring to be helps loosen the grip that the material world has on your mind. It is an immediate expression of the recognition of the equality of yourself and others.

Giving protection. Giving protection means becoming someone's safe haven, being their angel. Helping someone feel safe and helping them become safe are ways of offering protection. A friend of mine was once a trained receptionist with a sexual-abuse hotline. He volunteered at the hotline several hours a week. I asked him how he spent these few hours. He told me he sometimes supplied people with resources, but, he said, "Mostly, I listen. It is amazing how much safer someone feels when they have a witness, someone who just receives their suffering with compassion." Giving protection can be as simple as helping someone feel safe by listening with empathy.

Saving a life is another way to offer protection. A Tibetan lama once told me he was walking down a road in India when he saw a man leading a young goat. They exchanged a friendly greeting, and the lama asked him, "What are you doing with the goat?" The man answered that he was leading the goat to town to be butchered. The lama felt very compassionate toward this goat and bought it right then and there for a good sum of rupees. He kept it as a pet and cared for it for the rest of its life. Giving protection can be as literal as protecting an animal from the butcher's knife.

Offering protection can be as simple as helping someone feel less afraid. When a friend is sick, help him or her figure out what is wrong. Lend someone your umbrella in a rainstorm. Let someone bury their head in your arm at a scary movie.

Giving ease and comfort. One of the best ways to give is so simple that we never think of it: be at ease with yourself and with others. Ease is contagious.

Many of us have some degree of anxiety in social situations. We worry about how we come across, or what the other person is thinking, or any number of things. Or else we might be agitated by the thought that we had rather be somewhere else, doing something else, or with someone else. This takes us away from the present situation and opportunity to give in this moment. The next time you are around others, try the exercise of letting go of some of those thoughts; breathe and be at ease with yourself and others. Try a simple smile that says, *I am so glad to be here with you right here and now.* See what happens to your interactions with others.

One of the practice leaders and a spiritual guide in my Buddhist community is a college teacher. She gives ease by occasionally creating a "zone of peace" at her school (she calls it a "tea gathering"). She prepares tea for her coworkers in a pleasant space at the college where she works. She makes a conscious effort to create a space of peace and comfort where there is no gossip, just sincere listening and togetherness. By imagining the "zone of peace," she says that a remarkable sense of bonding has arisen among her coworkers through these meetings.

Giving ease also includes any nonmaterial giving that induces happiness and comfort. Consider a simple gesture like touching someone's arm or giving them a hug. Appropriate physical contact is a wonderful way to put someone at ease. Consider comforting someone who is grieving or worried. Consider music. Singing or playing an instrument for someone can ease their soul. Consider a smile. A simple smile can instantly confer ease and happiness to someone. As Mother Teresa said, "Every time you smile at someone, it is an act of love, a gift to that person, a beautiful thing." Being kind is a form of giving, perhaps the most profound form.

We may think we are not strong enough to offer any kind of comfort or real help to others. We may think we are not good enough to be a guide to others. Sometimes we allow our lack of self-esteem to act as an excuse for not offering guidance or comfort. We think, *I could not really act as a source of comfort to this person. I am not pure enough. I have my own problems.* That kind of thought is what keeps us from breaking through our rigid patterns of selfishness. Recognize it! Give yourself permission to be kind no matter what.

Offering encouragement. In your family, work environment, and community, people around you are striving to succeed, to learn, to make a difference, to contribute. Most of the time, we are focused on our own aims, goals, and projects. But if your purpose is to serve humanity, what is more important: your own aims and goals, or those of others? To serve humanity, you need to know what is important to other individuals, what they aspire to, and what they dream about. Try to observe and become familiar with what your family members, friends, and peers are working on, without judging or comparing it to what you value. What are their main projects? Once you notice what they care about, encourage them in their positive endeavors. About this form of giving, Shantideva said, "Having seen someone engaging in virtue, one should cheer him on with praises." Cheering someone on is a form of recognizing a person's potential. Pointedly encourage with specifics, instead of with "global praise" that can sometimes be ignored.

Exercise for Day Four

Give Verbally—Offering Encouragement

Today, look for an opportunity at work or in your home to offer encouragement. There are four steps to offering encouragement:

1. Notice when your friend, relative, or coworker is striving to accomplish something.
2. Consider what is important to your friend and why it is important.
3. Give up any jealousy or judgment you might be holding unconsciously.
4. Offer encouragement to the person before you, with a wish for his or her well-being and success.

Keep it simple. Does this verbal act change your subsequent interaction with that person? Does it change your state of mind? In what way?

Day Five

Paying Attention

The greatest gift you can give another is the purity of your attention.

—Richard Moss

Today's Date: _____

The phrase *paying attention* is interesting. It anticipates a relationship with the world in which we are contributing something tangible. What are we contributing to the world by paying attention? The act of being attentive is a form of "paying" our presence forward. When we are simply and directly attentive to another person—to their interests, their needs, their dreams, or merely to their presence—we offer them something lasting and deeply significant. As we continue to explore more ways to give, consider how paying closer attention to the people around you might enhance the act of giving.

Sharing knowledge. Offer your expertise. Be a consultant. Teach. You might be computer-savvy and be able to help a friend with computer problems. You might know a recipe that you can share with a neighbor. You might have a skill that you can teach to others. Notice what you have to share and offer it when possible. But share knowledge only if the gift will be appreciated. Sharing knowledge means not being stingy with your knowledge; it does not mean demonstrating your superiority over others. The Buddha never taught unless he was requested to teach, and even then he was circumspect. In the same way, you should not push your knowledge on others but find ways to share it sincerely in ways that benefit them.

Day Five

To share knowledge is a double gift. You share useful information, and you counteract the tendency to be selfish with what you know. You give away a bit of yourself.

Helping the sick. Where there is suffering, there is an opportunity to give. Being sick is never as simple as suffering from physical pain. Illness is accompanied by mental suffering, fear, anxiety, anger, and boredom. Serving people who are sick affords many opportunities for meaningful giving. Maybe this explains why many Buddhist saints studied medicine and helped patients, prior to or simultaneously with their dedication to spiritual pursuits. Gampopa, a great twelfth-century Tibetan saint, was called the Great Physician because he started out as a doctor. Kalu Rinpoche, my own teacher, trained in medicine in his early years under the guidance of his father (who was a doctor). As a child, he had no children's books: He learned to read from medical texts!

When my father became ill with cancer last year, he quickly began losing his independence. In a short span of time, he went from being able to walk for a hundred yards, to fifty yards, to ten yards. He lost his hair. He needed more and more morphine to stay comfortable. People began dropping by to pay their respects. He lives in a small farming community where everyone knows everyone else and treats each other like family. People from the community came by almost every morning for an hour or two. They would just sit in my father's room and make themselves available. I would come in to find them reading to him, helping him type on the computer, chatting with him about local news, changing his catheter bag, massaging his neck. One day, I asked my father how he liked these visits. "Oh, this is why I get up in the morning," he said. "If I get better, this love around me will be the reason."

A member of my spiritual community was treated for breast cancer last year. I asked her, of all the things her friends did to support her, what was the most helpful? She replied, "Oh. That is easy. Their *presence*. Having someone to accompany me to my doctor's appointments and treatments was good. But their presence was what it was all about for me." Sometimes just being there is the best gift we can give someone who is ill.

Repaying kindness. We live in a disposable and materialistic culture. Our economic models encourage people to think in terms of gain, loss, and exchange of labor. In school, even if we like a teacher, we might think, *Oh, but she is just doing her job. She is getting paid to teach us, after all.* When we are in a hospital, we might think, *The nurses and doctors are nice, but then again, they are getting paid to take care of me.* Once we have graduated from school or are out of the hospital, our tendency is to forget our connection to the people who assisted us. Our disposable culture encourages us to forget and move on to the next thing. In a culture in which material considerations are given such a high priority, the true kindness of those who serve us is often obscured by attitudes that focus not on the kindness itself but instead on imagined motives and materialistic considerations. We forget quickly, as if relationships are erased once we are no longer formally "in the system."

The first step to repaying kindness is simply to recognize the kindness that surrounds you all the time and has surrounded you your whole life. When you think of kindness, what do you think of? Kindness, we may think, is expressed by someone going out of his or her way to assist us. But what if we were to widen that definition in line with our life-intention, an intention that includes all humanity? What if we included all people who were *ever* kind to anyone in our list of kind people? So, for example, consider the teller at the bank who is in a snippety mood when you arrive at the window. That teller might not be kind to you right now, but if you think about it, perhaps she is a mother and is kind to her small child. If you and that child both have a wisdom-nature, what is the real difference to you whether you are the recipient of this teller's kindness, or the daughter is? In fact, when you think about it, since your job as a spiritual seeker is to serve others, it would be just as good or better if she lavished her kindness on someone else.

When you start to recognize kindness in its latent as well as in its manifest form, when you start to see the *potential* for kindness as just another form of *manifest* kindness, you develop a whole new perspective on everyone around you. You gain faith in humanity. You stretch your imagination and realize that everyone who has been kind to one member of humanity *has been kind to you*, albeit indirectly, because we are all connected. You give everyone the benefit of the doubt. The consequence of this kind of realization is that you become indebted to everyone. You owe all humanity for their various kindnesses—not to you, necessarily, but to others. They are assisting your project to serve others without even knowing it! Taking the wider attitude, Atisha, the great master credited with bringing the mind-training teachings to Tibet, said: "Be grateful to everyone." He included this aphorism in his verses for training the mind in loving-kindness.

Nevertheless, remembering specific kindnesses that have been shown to you in your life is also important. Who in your life has given you support? Who has fed and clothed you? Who has loved you and cared for you? Who has taught you what you know? Showing the people who have been kind to you that you remember and appreciate their kindness is one way to pay them back. Making kind and generous gifts to them is another way. Be courageous, and get used to expressing your gratitude to others.

Offering assistance. There is a famous king in Tibet known as Tang Tong Gyalpo who lived in the fifteenth century. This king was not famous for his politics, his policies, his economic savvy, or his foreign relations. He was remembered for literally building bridges, mostly bridges of iron. He built hundreds of sturdy iron bridges over the wide Himalayan rivers that run across the Tibetan plateau. Until then, crossing some of these swift rivers with treacherously steep banks had been a danger-ous matter, especially in the wet seasons. At that time, the technologies Tang Tong invented were revolutionary. No one had ever built bridges so sturdy and so lengthy. Some of these bridges are still safe crossings today. The far-seeing king is revered for helping generations of Tibetans get to the other side.

Tang Tong's bridges are a good metaphor for the role we play when offering assistance. Being an assistant to someone means thinking of yourself as a bridge over someone else's challenge, someone else's troubled waters, however small. No opportunity to help someone is too small to pass up. If you begin to think of yourself as a bridge, it will help you overcome your laziness in this regard. When you see someone needing help with something—groceries, lifting something, making a bed, house cleaning, washing the car, why not pitch in? Think: *I live to be a bridge.* Do not stand idly by watching people make efforts and struggle. Practice going to their assistance. Do not wait to be asked. Step up and help. See what it does to you. Remember, whether they really are in dire need of your assistance is not really the issue. If you are training to be a sage, being a bridge is part of awakening your wisdom-nature. There may be occasions when your assistance is not appreciated, and in those cases you should assess whether it is right to help. But generally, we hang back much more than we should.

This means keeping your radar up for those who need help. In addition to being a physical help to others, there are opportunities on occasion to be of verbal help. Some verbal forms of assistance include mediation, translation, deescalation of a volatile situation, giving directions to someone who is lost . . . there are so many ways we can use our speech to offer assistance. When you assist others in this way, you make way for progress. Therefore, be a friend, an assistant, an aide, a pal. Or as Ralph Waldo Emerson put it, "Be an opener of doors."

Listening. When you listen to someone else speaking, what does your mind generally do? Are you really attentive to the person in front of you, or is your mind wandering, composing a reply, engaged in your own mental chattering, passing judgment, coloring in your character profile of the person, or off on a tangent of memory? You can learn a lot about your ability to listen simply by noting what your mind is doing when you listen to someone else speak. It might help to consider three kinds of listeners. This model is loosely based on a Buddhist model of listening presented in the context of the way disciples listen to their spiritual guides.

The first kind of listener is like an upside-down plastic bowl. He is so distracted with his own thoughts and feelings, or the circumstances in his environment, that the words of the person in front of him run off him like water off a plastic bowl. He is not able to give the gift of deep listening because he is not fully present. He is more present with his own mental distractions and conceptual reactivity than with the person before him. The second kind of listener is like a salad bowl. She listens to the person in front of her and absorbs the words and meaning slightly, as an unvarnished salad bowl will soak up a little water poured into it. But she is somewhat distracted by her thoughts and feelings. Her thoughts are pulling her away from being fully present with the words of the person in front of her. Because of this distraction, her gift of listening is not completely realized. The third kind of listener is like an unfired clay pot. This kind of listener lets the words of the person in front of him fully penetrate his mind and feelings, in the way that an unfired clay pot soaks up water. His ears and mind are directed fully to the person in front of him. This kind of person is fully present and therefore capable of deep listening. What kind of listener are you?

Deep listening with pure attention is a profound gift. Think back to the times you have felt thoroughly listened to. Now reflect also on the times in your life you felt you were not being heard. Compare these two experiences. This is one way to understand how deep listening is a profound way to serve others. The next time you are with someone and listening to him or her speak, notice the quality of your attention. Are you listening deeply?

One of the biggest mistakes we tend to make when we listen is to want to "fix it," whatever it is. We think that we can either help fix it, or we cannot help at all. This is one of the greatest social mistakes we make every day, and it is the source of much of our social frustration and impatience. We are more caught up in orchestrating what we consider the ideal response or a "fix-it" response than we are on actually listening to what the other person is saying. As an alternative, the next time you talk to someone, consider that the best gift you have to give at that moment is not in the solution and not in your response: it is in listening and empathizing. It might be that you will be able to offer some real advice and assistance, but this help is impossible if it is not preceded by deep listening.

Giving victory to others. It sounds counterintuitive, but giving victory to others is one of the best gifts you can give. If you always have to be right, you will never be able to serve others to the fullest extent possible. Accepting blame and loss is one of the most profound methods for shifting the center from yourself to others. It takes some practice, but it is worth experimenting with.

Most of the time, when you really examine any given situation, there is no reason not to accept blame, even if you do not think you are blameworthy. Take the example of a time when you and your spouse (or a friend or a relative) are in the car driving to an unfamiliar place. You are reading the directions, perhaps written out by your friend. Somewhere along the way, you get lost. Your friend says to you something along the lines of, "It is your fault! If you were a better direction reader, we would not be in this mess!" You feel immediately irritated and uncomfortable. You feel defensive and mentally construct reasons you are not at fault. Your initial reaction is to point out that your friend wrote out the directions, not you. You were just reading them.

But why do we do this? Is it really because we are usually right? The truth is, in most situations, there is rarely an absolute right and wrong. There are always gray areas. The reason we shy away from blame is not because we are absolutely right and the other person is wrong, but because we cling to an ego, because we are fixated on what is ours: our opinions, our correctness, our things. The more strongly we cling to "me" and "my," the more we jump to defend them. That is why we become irritated and uncomfortable when we are blamed. We think that by accepting blame, we lose the battle.

And that is not far from the truth: our ego *does* lose the battle! However, that is not a reason to be irritated—it is a reason to celebrate. By offering victory to the other, you lose the little battle, but you win the big battle: the battle against your own selfishness. It takes a great deal more courage and flexibility to be willing to accept blame than it takes to fight for being right. In situations like the one described above, there is no reason whatsoever not to turn to your friend and say, "You are right! I am not a good direction reader. I got us into this mess. I am sorry. Let us see what we can do to get out of it." Cheerfully accepting blame takes practice. But it is one of the quickest ways to tame your ego, flatten arguments, smooth out tensions, and create peace. In truth, we have nothing to lose but attachment to our own agendas.

You might object to this and say, "But there is a time to fight!" You will reflect on times when you stood up for what you believed was right. Would it not be weak and even wrong to back down and let the other side win if you are truly right? Perhaps, if we could trust ourselves to be truly other-centered. Standing up for what is right for humanity and defending one's ego are two different things, and we are not very good at separating the two. Our selfish need to be right is generally stronger than our moral outrage.

The practice of giving victory to others helps chip away at your own selfish need to come out on top, and therefore it is a good way to develop the wisdom that separates a competitive impulse from one that stands up for others on the basis of love. So if you must fight, fight your urge to be right all the time. You need to start by battling your own ego and fixations before you can fight the big battles for the sake of those you serve, for the sake of your family, community, humanity, and all life. Once you get good at taking the blame, you can also become truly skillful at standing up for what is right, not because *you* think it is right, but because it is truly what is best for those you serve.

This method is so counterintuitive that Langri Tangpa, one of the great Tibetan teachers on methods of mind training, described it as "secret":

Give all victory to others; take defeat for yourself. . . . Employ this secret key!

This practice is a "secret key" in the sense that its benefits are not obvious through observation; the method has to be tried and repeated to unlock its benefits. Then you begin to understand what a profound method it is for taming our tendency to be self-centered. So the next time you feel blamed, try an experiment. One of my students put it this way: Take a deep breath, let the shoulders drop, exhale. Then step up to the plate and take responsibility for whatever situation or problems present themselves wholeheartedly and cheerfully. Give all the correctness to the other. If you want to flatten your self-centeredness, deescalate the situation, and create peace within yourself and with others, this is one of the most effective methods.

Now that you have looked over all these ways of giving, which one do you identify as the hardest way to give for you? Put a mark by that mode of giving. This is your target mode for the week. Be on the lookout for opportunities to exercise this way of giving in the next few days. If you know your body has a weak spot—a bad knee, for instance—and you are planning to climb a mountain, you would make a special effort to strengthen your knee before the climb. In the same way, tackle your weak points first. Why? Two reasons: first, the areas where you are weakest are also the areas where you have most room to evolve; and second, the areas where you are weakest are the areas where your spiritual journey is most vulnerable.

Day Five

Exercise for Day Five

Target a Way of Giving

Look over the ways of giving we discussed on Days Four and Five. Which do you identify as the hardest way to give for you? Write that mode of giving below.

My target mode of giving: _____

This week, work on this mode of giving. Be on the lookout for opportunities to exercise it in the next few days. How does it feel to give in this way? What did you discover?

Day Six

The Five Steps of Giving

Do not practice generosity looking for a result.

—Gampopa

Today's Date: _____

Many people think of themselves as basically generous, and the world may see them that way. Even if you do not perceive yourself that way, you are generous to some degree because you already give sometimes. Every time you do something for someone, you are giving. However, you probably do not usually think of giving as a spiritual practice. To give as a spiritual practice means to give consciously, to give with an awareness that the act of giving is a form of serving humanity in action. When you give consciously, you push your personal envelope of giving. Everyone's envelope looks different. No one can judge what becoming magnanimous means for you. You are your own best witness. The point is not to be a giver (you already are) but to increase your magnanimity quotient, to become someone who consciously works to evolve from an actor into a doer of deeds.

Dharma Tip

The attitude of magnanimity includes being kind and loving to yourself. This week, while practicing acts of giving, it is important to balance the generous impulse with practices of self-care. Practices of self-care include whatever leads to long-term well-being— such as eating right, exercising, meditating, and getting adequate rest—rather than short-term gratification.

Day Six

How does one move from haphazard giving to conscious and purposeful giving? One way is to follow the Five Steps of Giving, a formula for giving borrowed from the Buddha's teachings on karma. Having a formula helps us transform a haphazard activity into a conscious action—or, put another way, into a spiritual practice. When the Buddha taught about karma, he pointed out that any single purposeful action can be deconstructed into parts or steps. Before a person does something, there are conditions, motivations, and preparations. Then there is the act itself: the person carries out the action. Finally, there are repercussions: the completed action has results in the outer world and in the mind of the actor. This holds for any action, and it is true also for the act of giving. Having a formula gives you something to focus on when the opportunity to give presents itself. Since you are working on a target mode of giving—an unfamiliar or a hard mode—you will find this formula especially useful. It gives you an immediate plan of action to follow even when you are not inclined or feel at a loss for where to start.

1. Look for a need or an opportunity. Almost any need will do, even one you already address regularly (such as picking your daughter up from soccer practice). Better yet, discover a need that you have left hanging. What kind of assistance have you recently been asked for but not followed up on? What favor have you been asked for but have put off granting? We tend to procrastinate on favors if we see no particular benefit for ourselves. You should start here. If nothing comes to mind, then extend your mind to look for needs around you that you have not been asked to fulfill. Whatever you choose, keep it simple.

Sometimes, when you make an offering, such as when you give victory to another, there is no explicit need on the part of the recipient. Instead, your gift is made out of awareness of the best possible outcome for all concerned. While there is no need, there is a chance to make someone a little more comfortable, a little happier. There is a chance also for you to tame your selfishness.

2. Plan. Take one concrete step, even a small one, to address a need or take advantage of a chance to give. Consider the right time and the right place. Sometimes the plan is very short—maybe just a few seconds, especially when you see an opportunity to give spontaneously.

3. Give. Now do it. The action might be simple and easy. Just remember that what you give is not as important as *how* you give. Think about what giving magnanimously means to you. Give without attachment. You know yourself when you are at your best. Conjure up that person. And remember to give with humility. Giving something away does not make you a better person than the recipient. Do it with kindness and an open heart.

4. Do not expect thanks. Be process oriented, not outcome oriented. If you give with strings attached, you are not giving in the spirit of magnanimity; you are giving because you want something back. Instead, consider that you are giving because it serves your life-intention, and that is part of your spiritual path. If thanks come your way, however, graciously accept them.

5. Rejoice and dedicate. Once you have given, be glad about it—let it make your day. One of the most important aspects of a spiritual journey is taking joy in doing good things. If you regret giving something away, it would be better not to have given it in the first place. Mentally dedicate your action of giving to the fulfillment of your spiritual journey. As Gampopa said:

> All generosity practices should be dedicated to unsurpassable, perfect, complete awakening.

Aspire that this action be a cause for your awakening *and* the awakening of others.

Anyone can consciously undertake these five steps and begin to create an atmosphere of magnanimity in his or her life. As more people around you become the recipients of your generosity, your relationships with them will gradually change, and your happiness quotient will increase.

Exercise for Day Six

Flexing Your Generosity Muscle

Try following the steps for giving at least once today.

- *Look for a need:* Look for a way to offer something to someone or to a group, in one of the ten ways discussed in Day Four and Five or in some other way.
- *Plan:* Take the needed steps to plan the act of giving.
- *Give:* Give with an open heart.
- *Do not expect thanks:* Give with no strings attached.
- *Rejoice:* Be happy that you have given!

Day Seven

Spiritual Sacrifice

The wise see knowledge and action as one.
—Bhagavad Gita

Today's Date: _____

*E*arlier in this part I defined sacrifice as an act of giving in which there is give and take: you give a gift and willingly accept or receive the consequences, even if it means an inconvenience for you. In theory, the joy of sacrifice for the sake of humanity *sounds* good. But how far are we really prepared to go? How much are we willing to give up? For most of us, when we are really honest with ourselves, the answer is, not much. We are willing to endure a little inconvenience or pain so that someone else can be comfortable or happy, but we are not willing to endure much.

Why is this? Why are people who are willing to make big sacrifices so rare? One reason is fear. If there is one thing that every sentient being shares, it is a fear of pain and suffering. Consider what happens when you place your hand too near a flame. You do not even have to think about it! You withdraw your hand instantly. Fear of pain, loss, and suffering is one of our most basic instincts, and it rules us perhaps more than we would like to admit. But if we are going to make sacrifices joyfully for humanity, we must—at least to a degree—recognize and face our most basic fear instinct. Only when we face it and work with it will we be able to get some leverage between instinctual reactivity and the choices of a sage.

According to the Buddha's teachings, there is one sole root to our instinctual self-defensive fear. It is the same root that underlies selfishness, greed, anger, and attachment. The Buddha called this root *ego-clinging.* Ego-clinging is our tendency to believe in an inherently existent self that is essentially permanent, unchanging, and separate from the world around it. Even if your rational mind thinks, *I am changing all the time, I am connected to the environment and others, I know I am impermanent . . .* and so forth, your instinctual self does not believe it: It acts and reacts on the basis that the ego—the entity you label as "me"—will be around from one moment to the next, even for a long time. It acts as if the self were static and invincible. And it acts as if it were the most important self in the world. Its mode is self-preservation. It defends itself against "the other" and scrambles after its own happiness and comfort. This ego-clinging is the part of each of us that principally asks the question, *What is in it for me?*

If you were to put the whole spiritual journey in a nutshell, it would come down to replacing the voice that asks, *What is in it for me?* with a voice that asks, *What is in it for the world/humanity/him/her/them?* The whole spiritual path comes down to systematically sapping the power of ego-clinging and nurturing the power of selfless love and wisdom. All the practices in this book aim in that direction, including this week's exercise, Contemplation on Giving and Receiving. But Giving and Receiving especially aims at taming ego-clinging through the development of compassion and empathy. When you feel compassion, there is less room for self-centeredness. Where there is little self-centeredness, you will find that it becomes possible to face and release the instinctual self-defensive fear that has prevented you from making sacrifices willingly and joyfully.

Giving and Receiving is an exercise in imaginative sacrifice, motivated by the emotion of loving compassion. Remember the exchange aspect of sacrifice? When you sacrifice, you give something away and take on whatever inconvenience or difficulty might be a byproduct of that giving. In the Contemplation on Giving and Receiving, you go a step further. Motivated by empathy for another, you reimagine your body and mind as a channel, a funnel, a conduit that exists to transport happiness to others in the human family. In exchange, your body-and-mind conduit simultaneously draws in and dissolves the suffering of the human family. Have you ever seen those concrete tunnels at the beach that channel and direct the tide as it comes in and then goes out to sea? The practice of Giving and Receiving is like that: You are channeling the ebb and flow of a tide of visualized happiness and suffering in and out of your own body. On one level, you are learning to switch your happiness joyfully for another's pain. But on a deeper level, you imaginatively make the ultimate sacrifice: you give up self-centeredness and take on an other-centered attitude.

When you practice the Contemplation on Giving and Receiving, you will begin, as usual, with the Three Arrivals, your Awakening Prayer, and relaxing and breathing. Then you will visualize in front of you, in your mind's eye, a person you know who is having difficulties: illness, mental anguish, depression, anxiety, life problems. If you can think of someone you know and like, that is best to begin with, because initially it is easier to feel compassion for a friend. But if you can't think of anyone you know, choose someone with whom you have some contact, even if through the media or through acquaintance. As you become more practiced in this contemplation, you can select people you do not know, and eventually you should pick people you do not particularly like. Ultimately, our objective is equal compassion for everyone, but we need to strengthen our compassion muscle gradually.

As with last week's exercise for Day Seven "Contemplation to Awaken a Sage's Love" (page 156), try to see your someone as if he or she were standing in front of you in a dream, as vividly as possible. Now consider, *What would it be like to be this person? What would it be like to be in his or her shoes right now?* Really put yourself in his or her place. How would you feel? What emotions and thoughts would be going through your mind? As you imagine in this way, you will begin to empathize spontaneously with this person. You may have a moment when you think, *Aha! That is how she feels!* Let your compassion for this person grow, along with a heartfelt wish to do something for her. Let it increase to the point where you think, *I cannot stand by and watch her suffer! I must do something.* The more focused you are on the imaginative process, the greater your compassion will grow.

194

Now you are ready to engage in Giving and Receiving. The practice is coordinated with your breathing. As you inhale, imagine that you pull in your friend's suffering and pain in the form of a darkish smoke. This smoke dissolves into nothingness, into emptiness, at your heart. It is important to dissolve it into emptiness. You are not literally breathing in smoke! This is an imaginative process, a symbolic contemplation. The nothingness represents the ego's ultimate lack of inherent existence. You are imaginatively dissolving your friend's pain into your own ego-lessness.

As you exhale, imagine that you send out everything good you have to offer to your friend, in the form of clear, white light. If your friend is sick, you especially send him health. If your friend is depressed, you send her joy. If your friend has lost his home, you especially send him wealth. But you also send everything else your imagination can conjure up that you have to share and give to the world: your good fortune, your happiness, your health, your confidence, your comfort, your optimism, your possessions. Send everything you can think of out on the breath in the form of white light. Repeat the whole process again several times, at least ten times. You can count this on your fingers. Some people prefer to count on a rosary, or on what are now popularly called "power beads" (those bracelets are actually derived from Buddhist rosaries).

As you practice Giving and Receiving, keep the image of yourself as a conduit, as a channel for pulling in and dissolving pain and for sending out happiness and love. Feel yourself grow more and more happy as you imagine your friend becoming relieved of her pain. Feel yourself lighten up. You are lightening up because with every out-breath you relinquish the thought of "mine." You stop clinging to what you have. As your clinging loosens, you will feel fuller, lighter, and more content. When you are finished with the practice, take a moment to let the visualization of your someone dissolve. Rest the mind for a couple of minutes. Dedicate whatever benefit has come from the Giving and Receiving contemplation to your someone, to humanity, and to the fulfillment of your spiritual journey. Practice this contemplation a few times this week, until you receive the instructions for the Week Six meditation.

By conditioning your mind in this way, you prepare yourself to make actual sacrifices more and more joyfully. The remarkable thing about this contemplation is that the practice does the work for you. Even after the first or second time you do this practice, you will begin to feel a loosening of the hold of your fear instinct. How can you be afraid of pain when it is no longer personal? You will begin to feel the wall of defenses that you carry around become more malleable. How can you be defensive when the walls between self and other are an illusion? Over time, you will lose much of your hesitation about taking on inconvenience when it is for the good of those you serve. After all, what is inconvenient for your ego is convenient for your wisdom-nature.

Exercise for Day Seven

Contemplation on Giving and Receiving

- The Three Arrivals: Arrive with body, breath, and mind.
- Say your Awakening Prayer aloud.
- Relax and breathe.
- Visualize in front of you a person you know who is currently suffering from illness, mental anguish, or other difficulties.
- Now consider, *What would it be like to be this person?* Let your compassion for this person grow stronger and stronger. Feel your heart softening. Develop a heartfelt wish to relieve the person of suffering.
- Engage in pulling in pain and sending out love for a few minutes (at least ten breaths).

- Now imagine that the person before you dissolves. Rest the mind in a state of peace.
- At the end of the session, dedicate your contemplation to the cultivation of love and wisdom.

May I master the art of shifting the center and recognize
that every act counts.
Since magnanimity begins with generosity; may I look
for ways to give every day.
May I become a doer of deeds.

To make a deep mental path, we must think over and over the kind of thoughts we wish to dominate our lives.
                                                            —Henry David Thoreau

Week Six

Grow Your Assets: Trust, Contentment, Conscience, Integrity

Step six of your spiritual journey is to grow your spiritual assets by developing character traits that support your altruistic intention and the growth of wisdom.

In Chinese Buddhist folklore, there is a character named Hotei, sometimes known as the Laughing Buddha. He is the portly, jolly character you sometimes see around Buddhist temples and in trinket stores in Chinatown. According to legend, he carries around a big bag on his back full of candy for children, rice plants for the hungry, rodents for companionship, and all the suffering he has taken on for the world. He pulls out of his bag whatever might be helpful to the people he encounters. In exchange, he takes their suffering away. Hotei is a Buddhist Santa Claus.

For a spiritual life, we need to assemble a gear bag like Hotei's. Our gear bag should contain practices, personal strengths, precepts, coping skills, and interpersonal skills that assist our path to awakening and make that path a reality. Already we rely on positive values taught to us by our parents and teachers and acquired from our own experience. The practice of building a spiritual life requires us to develop skills that specifically help us live out our ideals of wisdom and compassion, skills that help us become more enlightened, kinder, wiser people. Once we have developed and identified some tools, we can train to become skillful in their use, knowing when and how to use them.

About seventeen hundred years ago, Trisong Detsun, one of the early kings of Tibet, invited a legendary Indian Buddhist sage to his court. At the time, Tibet was not a Buddhist country, but the king was interested in learning more about Buddhism and possibly in converting his people. This great sage, the progenitor of the Buddhist tradition in Tibet, was named Padmasambhava, which means "the Lotus-born One."

Padmasambhava (Padma, for short) did not simply hand over the Buddha's teachings to the king. Instead, he composed cycles of teaching just for Tibetans, and—at least according to general belief—hid his teachings in caves, in water, in the air, and under the ground all over Tibet. Because these teachings were hidden in such an unusual way, they are called "treasure teachings." They were literally buried treasure. Like the treasures in Hotei's bag, Padma's treasures were intended to be unearthed when the time and audience were ripe.

In one of these treasure caches, Padma wrote down a list of strengths he felt constituted a spiritual person's character. He called this list the Seven Spiritual Assets, which are developed and mastered on the path to awakening. They are called assets because they are like forms of spiritual wealth, a packet of spiritual currency available to fund and sustain the journey to enlightenment.

Padmasambhava's Seven Spiritual Assets are

1. Trust
2. Contentment
3. Conscience
4. Integrity
5. Self-discipline
6. Enthusiasm
7. Wisdom

The Seven Spiritual Assets are roughly sequential: the earlier ones are the basis for the later ones. But in reality, we can work on these all simultaneously, using them like tools, reaching for the ones that are needed in a given situation. This week, we will cover the first four, and next week we will cover the final three. As we go though them, think about which assets appeal to you personally and why. When motivated by good intentions, embraced by love, and accompanied by magnanimous actions, these seven assets will become a fundamental source of spiritual wealth and strength.

Day One

Trust

The one who understands much displays a greater simplicity of character than one who understands little.

—Alexander Chase

Today's Date: _____

A good number of the questions at any given Buddhist meditation retreat for beginners concern, in some way, the question of faith. What is it all about? What does it mean in the context of Buddhism? Many people come to Buddhism because they have heard it is nontheistic and highly philosophical. Atheists and agnostics are often drawn to these retreats. They have heard that Buddhist principles rely on analysis, logic, and empiricism. That is true, but beginners are still surprised and sometimes shocked to discover that there are many devotional practices and expressions of faith in the Buddhist environment.

Many people associate faith with naiveté at best and blind belief at worst. Many people think of faith as diametrically opposed to reason and therefore something not to be trusted. However, in the Buddhist context, faith is not necessarily opposed to reason; it is complementary to reason. It can even be said that faith without reason is not true faith, or that which is not tested is not to be trusted.

Faith does not have to be about belief. It can be about the intuitive and feeling side of us. One way to understand faith is as a form of trust, exemplified by that open-hearted state of being that most young children have naturally, if they are raised in a safe and loving environment. This kind of open-hearted state embraces the possibilities in others and is open to mystery and the unknown. Faith can be a state of existential trust.

This state of trust is important for the spiritual path in that it is like a key. It opens the mind to the possibility for growth and evolution. It is the opening aspect of trust that makes it a potential catalyst of spiritual development. If, for example, you are going to dedicate yourself to serving humanity, you have to be open to trusting the basic goodness in others. Or, put another way, you have to trust in humanity's potential. If you are going to dedicate yourself to a path of awakening, you have to trust your own basic goodness and trust that a path of development can unearth it. In the most general sense, to move forward on a spiritual journey you cannot live in a constant state of suspicion. You have to be open to possibilities. And that is one good definition of trust: a mind-state that is open to possibilities. If a mind is open, it is supple; it is flexible. An open mind is a mind that is poised to change and evolve.

Becoming a spiritual ingenue. One of my teachers used to tell a story about the power of trust. Once, long ago in Tibet, there was a wise woman, a *dakini*, who lived happily with her husband. *Dakini* is a Sanskrit word that means "woman who travels in space." That sounds very mysterious, but it basically means a woman with extraordinary qualities, one who is spiritually evolved. Some kinds of dakinis are troublesome or powerful. This woman, however, was a special dakini: she was exceptionally wise and compassionate.

This dakini was married to a man who was kind and stable, but he was not particularly bright. The woman loved her husband very much, so naturally she wanted to help him cultivate wisdom and intelligence. But how? She would try to get him to catch on to the simplest of concepts, and he would have trouble grasping her meaning. This troubled her not so much from the point of view of practical considerations, but because she felt that he had a potential for wisdom that was not being fulfilled. So one day, she devised a plan to help her husband develop wisdom by taking advantage of his greatest strength: his trusting nature. Although her husband was rather obtuse, he did not have an ounce of guile in him.

Day One

The astute wife suggested to her husband that he spend one entire night at a local temple praying in front of a statue of Manjushri, the deity of wisdom. "If you pray fervently," she told him, "Manjushri himself will hand you something to eat in the morning. This food will bestow on you Manjushri's wisdom blessing. Take it in your mouth and swallow it." The husband trusted his wife deeply, so he did just as she suggested. While he prayed, his wife spent the night secretly hidden behind the statue, waiting. It must have been a long night for the two of them!

When the sun rose, the husband finished his prayers and then stretched out his hand toward the statue. His wife quickly reached around and placed a small dried apricot in the palm of his hand. With deep reverence, thinking the fruit had come from Manjushri—the deity of wisdom himself—he ate it. His mind was so convinced that the fruit was charmed with Manjushri's blessings that his intelligence instantly woke up.

When he returned home, he felt like a different person. He picked up some religious texts and began to study them. He soon became a great scholar. The catalyst for all this change was not really the apricot, of course, but rather the openness of his ingenuous mind. He was not incapable of developing wisdom—he just did not believe he was capable of it. The apricot was his spiritual placebo.

As this story illustrates, sincere trust is powerful enough to catalyze an awakening experience. To be successful on a spiritual journey, it helps to have some wide-eyed innocence, like the husband does in this story. Then when we meet our particular spiritual placebo, we will be open to any possibility, ripe and ready to awaken. We might wonder if this is not just being naive; but in a way, that is the point: if you are a little naive, you have a fresh mind. You are ready to wake up.

Have you ever noticed the trusting nature of young children? I recently reunited with a niece of mine whom I had not seen since she was an infant. She is now four years old. At first she was wary of the new auntie. But within about an hour, she was sitting on my lap, stroking my hair, taking me around by the hand, and singing to me. Most children, if they have grown up feeling safe, are naturally trusting and affectionate in this way. What happened to that child in all of us? Where is that spontaneous, open, wide-eyed, trusting little soul we once were?

We still have that trusting soul within. Getting back in touch with her reminds you to be a spiritual ingenue. Spiritual innocence, being willing to begin again every day, puts truth within your grasp. Perhaps the most profound secret of the spiritual path is that the deepest wisdom is profoundly innocent.

Is wisdom a kind of nonworldliness? Not exactly. It has to do with the nature of truth. Truth is not—in the wisdom traditions of the East—understood with conceptual cognition; it is perceived intuitively. Intuition is spontaneous and simple. It does not awaken easily in a mind that is cluttered with plans, ideas, and concepts. It awakens most easily in a mind that is receptive, fresh, and flexible. Truth awakens in the mind of a spiritual ingenue, not in the mind of an "expert."

Consider what happens when you think you know something. As soon as you think you have mastered it, you have really got it down, what happens? You conclude and wrap up. You think, *Oh, now I get it!* and—to some degree—you feel like the learning process is over. You begin to think of yourself as a finished product. In other words, when we "know" something, we enter a state of rigidity. A rigid mind is less susceptible to spiritual insight. So it pays to revisit your child's mind now and then and step into the clothes of a spiritual ingenue. For such a person, the big questions never grow old, and the quest is as new every day as the first day she started.

Devotion. I like to think of devotion as an equation. If it were a math problem, devotion would equal trust plus love. Devotion is a deep trust that is both intense and saturated with feeling. It can be a great destroyer of barriers and a great help to developing unconditional love. Reading between the lines of the story about the dakini and her husband, you can sense a bond of devotion—between wife and husband, and between the husband and the deity of wisdom. If the husband had not deeply trusted his wife, he would not have followed her suggestion to pray all night in front of a statue of Manjushri.

But the husband did have faith in his wife's wisdom and foresight and therefore believed that what she had to tell him was of real value. His trust in his wife was the impetus for the crumbling of the walls between himself and the deity of wisdom. His wife, in a sense, melted his boundaries. Likewise, his wife had a deep and abiding devotion to her husband. How else could she have believed in his potential to develop perfect wisdom? What else could have kept her up all night hiding behind a statue? She did not merely trust her husband—she trusted and loved him deeply.

What does it mean to be devoted? Being devoted means trusting what is deepest in yourself and others. It means plumbing the depths of the mystery that is you and that is others also. It means trusting the treasure beneath the crust: trusting the wisdom-nature in yourself and others. Devotion is what happens when you move toward integrating what you know about wisdom-nature with how you trust. When you have devotion, you cannot put much stock in appearances. Instead, you dive down beneath what people say, or how they behave, to believe in their inner purity and potential.

Almost everyone has some experience with the power of devotion in relationships. If you deeply believe in the goodness of a single person and love that person, does it not change your outlook on the whole world? It becomes easier to trust others, easier to forgive them, easier to love them. The presence of devotion in your life has the potential to bond you more securely to all of humanity.

In spiritual circles, a spiritual teacher, an embodied image of enlightenment such as the Buddha, or even sacred objects sometimes provide an outlet for that energy of devotion. At its best, that energy softens up patterns of rigidity and fear, making it easier for us to let others in and let our love out. You become willing to take risks for serving others that you would not take if you were inhibited by fear.

One of my teachers sometimes invoked the image of the sun shining on a snow mountain. An inflexible and isolated mind is like the snow mountain. The sun of devotion melts the mental stiffness that keeps others at a distance. It dissolves our rigid habit patterns, helping us transcend the limited sense of self and commit more fully to serving others. Then a river of magnanimous deeds for the benefit of humanity can more freely come into the world.

✦✦✦

Exercise for Day One

Meditation to Awaken Freshness of Mind

Try this meditation. Sit on your cushion and reflect, *This moment now is the only moment.*

Enter into a state of "young mind": Remember the state of mind you had as a young child, or imagine it, if you cannot remember. Sit as if you were experiencing every moment, every sound, and every thought for the first time.

Let yourself settle into a place of "not knowing," with simple, pure experiencing, in which you suspend assessments and judgments.

Day Two

How to Trust Wisely

Believe nothing, no matter where you read it or who said it, no matter if I have said it, unless it agrees with your own reason and your own common sense.

—The Buddha

Today's Date: _____

ave you had the experience of feeling betrayed by your own trusting nature, feeling that you trusted and were let down? For most of us, trust sometimes reveals a dark side: vulnerability. If we trust in the wrong way, or we trust the wrong person, we become vulnerable. Where we place our trust and how we trust seems to matter. That is why the Buddha recommended that a spiritual seeker should not trust blindly but should learn to trust wisely. We need to be smart about the where, who, and how of trust. Can the object of your trust be expected to stay the same forever? So often we all trust as if that were the case. If that really were so, we could trust pretty much anything. But that is not our general experience. Circumstances change. People lose their half of the commitment. Institutions crumble. New ones are born. Our own feelings cannot even be relied on! How do we deal with all the elements of constant change and still maintain the trust necessary to love like a sage, to reach out like a sage, to be devoted like a sage?

The Buddha helped us out by suggesting that spiritual seekers need to differentiate between what is _provisionally_ trustworthy and what is _ultimately_ trustworthy. Things that are _provisionally_ trustworthy include whatever and whoever helps you on the spiritual path. These the Buddha called the _dharma_ and the _sangha_. "Whatever helps you" refers to material and nonmaterial things that uplift you and move you forward on your spiritual journey, including books, practices, teachings, thoughts, and even events. These resources, broadly understood as dharma, can be trusted because they—in one way or another—facilitate your awakening. "Whoever supports you" is the sangha. Traditionally, during the Buddha's time, the sangha meant spiritual community. But in this day and age and in this global environment, I think it makes sense to consider all the people who support you on your spiritual quest as sangha, in some sense. Not everyone around you gives you direct encouragement in your spiritual endeavors, but your family, friends, coworkers, and so forth do give you the essential support and care you need to live up to your wisdom potential. The people who are a supportive presence in your life can be trusted because their presence makes it possible for you to fulfill your intention to serve others.

With this as a guide, it becomes easier to seek out who and what you can trust. But even so, the Buddha put the word *provisional* on that trust. Why provisional? Because as wonderful, precious, and essential as trustworthy objects and people are in our lives, there is an impermanent and fluid nature to everything. The Buddha used this example: The dharma (everything that sustains a seeker on the path to enlightenment) is like a boat that carries that seeker across the river of existence. When a seeker gets to the other shore—symbolizing enlightenment—would he pick the boat up on his shoulders and continue to carry it around? No. Would the people with him (the sangha) continue to walk in the same direction? No. The dharma will have served its purpose. The boat, so useful for river travel, becomes a burden on land. The people, as much as the seeker may love them, will eventually go their separate paths. This is the way of things.

This example would seem to mean that everything we rely on is destined to fall apart and disappear eventually. That is almost the case, but not quite. We still have one thing with us throughout the spiritual journey that will not depart. That one thing is the only thing that is *ultimately* trustworthy: the wisdom-nature itself. The Buddha put it this way: we can trust *buddha* ultimately. Did he mean we could trust him, the human being? He did not mean that. *Buddha* is Sanskrit for "Awakened One." The human Buddha meant that in the end, we can always take refuge in buddha-ness . . . enlightenment itself. That—along with its potential, the wisdom-nature—we can trust, because enlightenment is deathless and not subject to change. In other words, we can have full confidence in wisdom and our potential to develop it.

This is a bright thought when it comes to understanding people, including ourselves. It comes back to the old theme that we can trust most people provisionally, but we can trust the wisdom-nature in all people ultimately. Or put another way, a person can lead you astray, but the deepest part of any one person can never lead you astray. If you know how to differentiate between what you trust in her (or yourself) provisionally and what you trust in her (or yourself) ultimately, you will have a much easier time with relationships.

Okay, once you have an idea of what you can trust, how do you go about trusting? The Buddha helped us out here too by suggesting that trust is not a matter of diving in with both feet without looking. Trust is, and should be, developmental. A trust that develops over time becomes authentic and certain. This is the difference between trust and belief. You can contrive belief, but you cannot contrive authentic trust. Authentic trust is real, open hearted, and sincere. But it is not blind. It is backed by experience, analysis, and eventual certainty.

The Buddha taught that there are three developmental stages of trust: intuition, confidence, and certainty. When you first encounter something—let us say an idea, an environment, or a flesh-and-blood person—you have an intuitive reaction. You may think, *I feel really comfortable with this. I trust it.* Or you may think, *I do not trust this.* Or you might be intrigued but unsure, thinking, *I kind of trust this, but I have my doubts.* We have some kind of intuitive reaction to a first encounter with something, based on our past experiences, our personality, our values, and so forth.

Or sometimes it feels more mysterious than that. A Buddhist would say we react on the basis of our past karma with this idea or person—we are drawn toward or away from it on the basis of previous exposure.

In any case, in the early stages of an encounter with something or someone, we are in the intuitive phase of trust. That is your baseline feeling. It is only a feeling, not knowledge. Sometimes that feeling is really worth listening to. But you cannot be sure. An initial encounter is sometimes deceptive.

Therefore, you need to go further. You need to test this intuitive feeling. The next level of trust—confident trust—develops on the basis of experience, examination, and deduction. After you have encountered this person or thing, you go through a process of testing it. When it comes to testing a person, one of my lamas used to suggest asking two questions: Is the person nondeceiving, and is the person compassionate? I have found these criteria extremely helpful in my own life. To explore whether a person is nondeceiving and compassionate, you might ask yourself whether you see signs of dependability. Does the person seem honest, transparent, reliable? Does this person care about others, and is he or she moved by suffering?

If, instead of a person, the Buddha's students encountered an idea or concept, he advised them to test its logic. I myself found it useful to test ideas against empirical and deductive evidence. I was a feisty college student when I first encountered Buddhism, and I was far from accepting anything just because I was told to accept it. So I was glad to find a tradition that approved of scrutiny. Before you become confident about an idea, you should ask, *Does this idea hold up to examination? Does it make sense? Does it ring true? When I try it out, does it work? Why or why not?* The Buddha encouraged his own disciples again and again to question his own teachings in this way.

Once you have thoroughly examined a set of ideas, if they stand up to your scrutiny you begin to move from a trust based on feeling to a trust based on confidence. Your trust is still deductive, not direct, but you become confident at this phase. It is not a sign of disrespect to put an idea or person through a little background check—it is a sign of respect. We value him, her, or it enough to devote our energy to some examination.

Finally, you reach the third phase of trust. In ordinary life, we usually go through only the first two phases of trust, and we do not have access to a third phase. But in spiritual life, you gain access to the possibility of a trust that is elevated above confidence. The third phase of trust—certainty—cannot be achieved through logic or analysis. It can only be achieved through bringing wisdom into the encounter. In meditation and through contemplation, over time, you will directly *experience* your own nature. On the basis of directly experiencing your own nature, you will spark insight into the nature of the world around you. When this kind of insight is brought into an encounter with an idea or a person, what to trust becomes absolutely clear, without doubts or uncertainties. You will recognize, from your own direct experience, the truth present in the idea or the other person. In a way, you come back to working with intuition, but now it is with a much deeper form of it.

So, absolute trust in people or ideas is tied to insight. Once you glimpse absolute truth directly, your trust settles on the underlying truth in any idea or set of ideas. Your trust settles on the deepest part of whomever you meet. If you meet buddha in yourself, like the pilgrim who saw his own reflection, you cannot look at others without seeing the Buddha in them, as well. In sum, the asset of trust is both a support and a litmus test for how well you are mining the gold of your own wisdom-nature.

Exercise for Day Two

Relative and Ultimate Trust

Take some time to consider: *What and who in my life do I trust? Why?* Write down the names of three things [or people] you trust provisionally and why you trust them.

Things/people I trust provisionally:

1. _____

2. _____

3. _____

What can you trust ultimately? What can you trust that will never leave or deceive you? Write this down in your own words:

_____

_____

Day Three

Contentment

The tighter you squeeze, the less you have.
                                    —Thomas Merton

Today's Date: _____

There is a Buddhist saying: "Contentment is the greatest wealth." *Contentment* in Tibetan is *chok shepa*, literally, "knowing enough." It means being satisfied with whatever you have, knowing that you do not need that new car, that big house, that person to make yourself content. Spiritual contentment implies being carefree, unattached, and unencumbered. It means having an ability to hold things lightly. No matter how much money you might have, how much property you own, or what luxuries you indulge in, if you do not hold them lightly, all these things become burdens. Without contentment, even the tycoon on his tropical island suffers.

The other day I was taking a walk with one of my students. He recollected that just a few years ago he was a destitute college student. He had so little money that he literally had to keep track of every penny. He was always worried about money. After college, he got a job that paid fairly well. For the first time in his life, he was able to save some money. He expected things would get easier, but that is not what happened. He had money, but now he was constantly worried about losing it!

Does this not sound familiar? Our minds believe that suffering originates from not having enough. But when we get what we need, we still manage to be discontent. Why? The suffering does not come from lack. It does not come from overabundance, either. It comes from attachment. It is the clinging mind, the emotionally involved mind, that

215

makes us miserable. It is the sense of trying to hold on to whatever we have that weighs on our heart and makes us feel strangely destitute. Whatever you have will always feel heavy if you do not cultivate an internal sense of lightness about the material world, a sense of being content with however much or little you have.

Tibet was a rough place to live. Because of the cold and high altitudes, there was little to eat even in the best conditions. Therefore, many of the great yogis of Tibet excelled in the practice of cultivating contentment. It was an environmental imperative. One such yogi was the cave-dwelling ascetic Lorepa. For twelve years, he meditated on an island in the middle of Lake Namtso in northern Tibet. This lake freezes over in the winter, and Lorepa did not have a boat, so he often spent many months completely isolated, seeing no one. One autumn, he ran so low on resources that he was forced to boil his leather shoes and meditation belt for food. Still, he was unworried and cheerful, supported by the power of contentment and his great enthusiasm for meditation practice.

How can someone like Lorepa remain carefree and happy in conditions that would depress most of us? Lorepa's method of developing contentment relied on a practice called "equal taste." Equal taste means recognition of the basic sameness of all things. The implication is that all things, including experiences and feelings, are permeated by a common nature or truth that can be "tasted" by a person's wisdom. Lorepa strove to see the equal taste, or the basic sameness, of happiness and suffering. Instead of getting carried away with the usual reaction to hardship—i.e., suffering—he discovered, through his meditation practice, that suffering was of the same *essence* as happiness. Likewise, instead of getting carried away with the usual reaction to comfortable circumstances—happiness—he discovered that happiness was of the same essence as suffering. On the surface, suffering and happiness appear different, but at their core is a single taste, a single essence that transcends difference. This is a profound insight cultivated in the practice of some advanced meditations in the Tibetan tradition. Because Lorepa had meditated a lot on the equal taste of happiness and suffering, he was able to be perfectly content in any situation no matter how difficult, even when eating his shoes!

Dharma Tip

Many dharma practices, such as the exercise for Day Three of this week, require looking into your everyday experiences in new ways. It is often difficult to remember to do this or even what to do at first. Buddhist monks traditionally memorized instructions (in verse form) to remind themselves what to do. For us, one way to remember is to carry around the instructions (copied over or photocopied) and use them for reference when we practice. After a short time, you will memorize the instructions, and it will become easier to practice spontaneously.

Mastering the practice of equal taste takes years of meditating under the guidance of an experienced master. But you can get an idea of the beneficial power of equal taste by trying this exercise. Sometime when you are feeling unhappy, discontent, or depressed, turn inward and look directly at the mind that is discontent (nothing special, just the sense of *I* in the sentence *I feel unhappy*). Ask yourself, *Who is discontent? Who suffers?* Try to face directly the one who feels, not the feeling. Look at the "who." Then, at another time when you are feeling happy and content, turn inward and look directly at the mind that is happy. Ask, *Who is happy? Who is content?* Look directly at the one who feels happiness, not the happiness itself. Look at the experiencer of happiness.

You may need to try this exercise a few times, maybe even many times, before you feel comfortable with it. But after awhile, you start to notice something peculiar and astonishing: The "who," the experiencer, does not change. While the object of your attention changes, and the feeling changes, the knower of the feeling, the perceiver of happiness or suffering, the experiencer, is fundamentally the same person, the same mind. Some deep and fundamental part of yourself, your mind, remains constant throughout all experiences. Becoming familiar with this basic experiencer of everything is a good exercise in approaching equal taste, because it allows you to take a step back from the experience. It gives you a refuge.

Exercise for Day Three

Self-Observation

This exercise will be done not on your cushion but rather over the course of the day. It involves looking at your mind when you are in particular moods.

- First, at a time when you happen to be feeling happy or content, turn inward and look at the quality of the "self" experiencing happiness. Do this exercise without a preconceived notion of what you will find. See if you can look beyond the feeling, the state itself, to the fundamental core of the experiencer, the mind itself.
- Then, at another time, when you happen to be feeling depressed, worried, irritated, or unhappy, do the same: look inward at the "self" experiencing unhappiness. Try to look beyond the feeling to the one experiencing suffering.
- At the end of the day, take some time to assess: Is your mind when you are discontent fundamentally different from, or the same as, your mind when you are happy? Is the one who is experiencing happiness the same person/mind as the one who is experiencing unhappiness? Is there something there that remains stable and unchanging throughout both happy and sad experiences and is untouched by them?

Day Four

Appreciation

The roots of all goodness lie in the soil of appreciation for goodness.

—Dalai Lama

Today's Date: _____

*I*n developing the asset of contentment, ironically, discontent is a good friend. Why is that? While subtle discontent is hard to recognize, obvious discontent is not. Obvious discontent makes itself known to us with a familiar voice, the internal diatribe. You know the one: the private complainer, the inner lawyer, the hidden Scrooge, the occasional monologue that starts up seemingly of its own accord when things do not go your way. On your spiritual journey, that voice is a helpful internal compass. Without it, it is hard to see our discontent. The internal voice that finds fault with everything is a mirror of the discontented mind. That reflection is a spiritual angel, because it tells you loud and clear that now is the time to practice contentment.

How do you do that in the midst of an internal diatribe? Two methods are favorites of mine. The first is the path of analysis, of reasoned reflection. It comes from the great master Shantideva. Instead of obsessing over what you are not content with, take a moment to ask yourself one simple question about what you are obsessing over: *can I do anything to change this for the better?* If the answer is yes, then there is no point in obsessing over it, is there? There is a point in actively changing it for the better, but nothing is accomplished by complaining. If the answer is no (and much of the time it is), there is especially no point in obsessing. There is a point in accepting it, but no point in complaining about what you cannot change.

The second method is to take a quick break from your diatribe to notice something. This outer situation is not the cause for the diatribe; the inner situation is. Tilopa, a great Indian Buddhist master, put it this way to his disciple Naropa in a famous verse: "Do not suppress appearances, Naropa: Cut attachment!" What makes us suffer and complain is not him/her/it but our own grasping at appearances. It is worth a moment of suspicion to root out your own participation in the deal. When you get an inkling that *you* are the fuel for your internal monologue, it becomes fairly easy—well, at least easier—to change the content of the inner talk.

First, consider the relativity of the situation. What seems repulsive to you is not so to someone else. What seems a big hassle to you is some-one else's tiny bump in the road. And in the grand scheme of life, what is this little moment anyway? Try to step out of the situation for a minute and see it from another point of view, or take the long view of a lifetime. When you are on your deathbed, is this what you will remember? Is this what you will want to remember?

Second, consider that the monologue is fueled not by the situation but by clinging to facets of the situation. It is as if the mind were sticky with a glue that keeps us adhering to, obsessing over, subjects and top-ics—whatever is in front of us. If your mind is going to be sticky, you can choose what you want it to stick to. Pause your monologue and take an "appreciation break." Take a moment to detach and refocus on the things you usually overlook about your life. Think about the people in your life whom you cherish. What would life be like without these people and these things. If you have to obsess, *appreciate obsessively*. Mentally enumerate what you have in this very moment. This is time well spent. Even when you are not in a diatribe moment, it will make you a lot more content.

Day Four

Exercise for Day Four
Take an Appreciation Break

- Take a break from what you are doing and leave aside what you were thinking about.
- Breathe and close your eyes.
- Think of three simple things about your life that you are grateful for. Maybe even write these down.
- Consider what life would be like without these three things.
- Allow gratitude to fill your heart. Relax into a sense of contentment. Bask in the sun of appreciation!

Day Five

Conscience

This is the very perfection of a man, to find out his own imper-
fections.

—St. Augustine

Today's Date: _____

The third spiritual asset is conscience. The Tibetan word for conscience is *ngo tsa* (I know it looks hard to pronounce!). It literally means "hot face," and it refers to blushing. The word suggests an automatic emotional response related to a sense of shame, not ordinary shame but its enlightened counterpart: a sense of conscience. Conscience is an awareness of one's duty to others over and above selfish concerns. Conscience, as a spiritual asset, is a moral radar that intuits right and wrong. Since a spiritual journey is focused on serving humanity, intuiting right and wrong comes down to intuiting the line between help and harm.

In the biography of Milarepa, the great ascetic yogi of Tibet, Milarepa and his sister, Peta, have a debate of sorts about conscience. Milarepa spent his entire life in the remote caves of Tibet, devoting himself entirely to the spiritual path. In many ways, he is the model of the sage who is determined to follow the path to awakening without a single distraction. He shunned villages, lived on wild nettles, and begged for the occasional bag of barley. Although Milarepa lived in the eleventh century, his fame lives on to the present day through his lively biography and spiritual songs.

Peta was not happy with Milarepa's choice of lifestyle. He went naked most of the time. To all conventional appearances, he seemed a bit like a madman. Even in Tibet, where such asceticism was somewhat acceptable, he was an anomaly. Underneath his feral appearance, however, he was cultivating unconditional love for all beings, profound wisdom, and deep meditation. But Peta could not see why the asceticism was necessary. Her brother could be a rich Buddhist priest down in one of the Tibetan villages. If he would just clean up his act, he would be an object of local veneration! She was sure his pride in his extreme asceticism had clouded his vision. Still, she loved her brother and brought him food regularly. Her hope was that she would be able gradually to civilize him, convince him to give up his one-pointed quest, and recruit him to a more urbane standard of living.

To start the process, one day she brought him a cloth that she herself had painstakingly woven out of goats' and sheep's hair. While a wool garment was not a fine robe, exactly, it was modestly respectable attire, she thought. Keeping her face turned away in embarrassment, she begged him, "Please at least make a loincloth out of this. I cannot stand to see you naked!" Then she handed the cloth to her brother and went away.

While she was gone, Milarepa cheerfully cut up the cloth. He made a hood for his head and little hats for each of his ten fingers and ten toes. And finally—the pièce de résistance—he made a sheath for his penis. Why not? It was his extremities that got cold in the harsh climate, not his torso.

When his sister returned, she turned deep red with outrage. She was trying so hard to civilize her brother, and look at him! Here he sat on a rock in front of his cave looking like a wild banshee, with a hood over his head, and little hats for all his extremities, and even a little sheath for his . . . oh, my! He might have seemed a little peculiar before, but now?

"Brother, have you no shame?!" she cried in exasperation, averting her eyes.

"What?" Milarepa replied. "Is it that I have clothed my member so artistically? It is, after all, just a natural extension of my body. I was born with it! What about your female organ—are you ashamed of that? You blush, but it seems to me there are more relevant things to feel ashamed of. The world is upside down! People feel shame about what

223

is decent and proud of what is shameful. What should really bother our conscience is indulging in harmful actions and acting with hypocrisy. If you are going to feel indignant, why focus on my entirely natural body parts? Pay attention to what is truly worth feeling indignant about!"

Do you not love it that siblings have always been siblings? But, as light as the story may be, Milarepa was also giving Peta a profound and subtle instruction in the meaning of spiritual conscience. Milarepa's point was that shame can be well placed or misplaced. Misplaced shame is a sense of shame about superficial appearances. Well-placed shame is spiritual conscience: a sense of concern about whether you are serving a wise intention. Peta was so focused on Milarepa's appearance that she failed to see the selfishness of her own agenda. Are we not all like that much of the time? Consider the news stories covered in any given day: many of them are just for the shock value. We love to shake our heads. We love to be outraged. We love to criticize, as long as the criticism is not directed at ourselves. That is what Milarepa meant when he said, "The world is upside down!" A person of conscience does not find the superficial appearances of the world difficult to tolerate—he finds his own deviations from love and compassion difficult to bear.

But there was another lesson here for Peta. She was so focused on society's norms (norms that her brother never considered at all normal) that she could not see the larger spiritual project that Milarepa was engaged in. Milarepa did not care if he was mocked by rich villagers. He was not concerned at all with what society thought of his appearance— he cared more about the good of humanity. He was interested in doing what was right and just in the big picture, not in what was acceptable in the little picture.

In that way, Milarepa embodied a trait we see in so many of this century's most popular heroes: Gandhi, Susan B. Anthony, Martin Luther King, Jr., and Desmond Tutu, to name just a few. None of these heroes considered society's norms to be at all *normal*. What they considered to be normal was an ethic of justice that sometimes goes entirely against the norms of society. From a spiritual perspective, one might say that justice is whatever upholds the welfare of all humanity. Injustice is whatever harms that welfare. Cruelty, oppression, violence, indifference, apathy . . . a person of conscience is not interested in how these play out for him or her alone; a person of conscience feels how these play out for humanity. Seeing the bigger picture makes the blood rise for a person of conscience. A sense of justice—how things *should* be in the world—puts the blush in enlightened shame. Conscience cannot witness injustice in society and turn the other way, because in some way society *is* the body of a sage. We may not feel that connected now, but we become more that way every day we focus on the intention to serve others.

Conscience is a moral compass, a radar. It is a sense of moral fortitude, an ethical vigilance, a sense of right and wrong, a decency check. Developing conscience means finding your moral center. When you find that center, you enter a space of reflection: you pause. The moment of conscience is a pause in the pattern of reactivity, a pause in which to choose the right path and to act on the basis of your values, not on the basis of habit. Since injustice is defined by whatever harms the welfare of humanity, developing conscience means stopping to ask, *How does this action (or these words) affect those around me? Is anyone harmed by this? Is anyone harmed by my inaction?* When you begin to ask these questions, you move into the space of discovering a profound companion to conscience: spiritual gentleness. The Buddha and Gandhi called it *ahimsa*. You can see the commitment to spiritual gentleness reflected in the dedication to nonviolence and peace that characterizes many popular advocates of peaceful resistance.

There is a Buddhist saying, "If you cannot help, at the very least, do no harm." This reminds me of the Hippocratic Oath: "I will prescribe regimens for the good of my patients according to my ability and my judgment and never do harm to anyone." In some ways, Hippocrates and the Buddha took a similar stance on service. If your mission is to serve others, helping others is not all you need to consider. If you run full tilt at helping but forget to refrain from harming, you may not be of much help. You have heard variations on the phrase, "Harry has good *intentions* . . ." We recognize that as a euphemism meaning that Harry builds one bridge and burns ten. We do not want to be like that.

If instead we can avoid harming others as much as possible, if we can be truly gentle and nonviolent, that is paramount to helping. That alone is an accomplishment of a lifetime.

That does not mean that choices are always easy—the most dedicated spiritual seekers face moral dilemmas. Almost every day, we are faced with choosing between lesser harms. The Indian master Atisha, a Buddhist advocate of spiritual gentleness, remarked that he found it very tough always to stick to his vow to serve all others and refrain from harming them. And this was a sweet, innocuous monk who had hardly a chance to harm others in the way we might normally think of harm! For this reason, he again and again renewed his heroic intention, every day reminding himself of his vow. If Atisha was challenged by the vow to refrain from harm, we certainly will be. Nevertheless, Atisha also left us with a profound insight: Outer appearances mean less than your inner attitude. You are your own best witness. If your decisions are informed by love and wisdom, if they are toned with gentleness, you are more likely to do the right thing—at least the best you know how to do at that moment.

One of my favorite descriptions of spiritual gentleness comes from Atisha: "Make your mind soft like cotton wool." Cotton wool is the very soft, silky fibers of cotton in its raw state. Have you ever touched raw cotton? It is pleasant to touch and yields to the slightest pressure. What Atisha meant is this: make your mind yielding, warm, sensitive, and pleasant to others. He meant soften your hard edges. Think for a moment about your hard edges—what are the parts of you that put a wall between yourself and others? Be specific in your thoughts. Think of a specific interaction recently where you felt your barriers go up in an uncomfortable way. Now try to put a label on your pattern. Some examples: *I have a tendency to withdraw in social situations; I am easily irritated by people who have beliefs that differ from mine*; and so forth. Cynicism, a temper, emotional coolness, a tendency to be defensive, fear of social situations, sarcasm? We all have some mechanisms that deflect intimacy and connection with others and are likely to impede a spiritual mission that is all about relationship and compassion.

These mechanisms are a bit like an armadillo's hard shell. We think of them as self-protection. But while we think of them this way, our hard edges do not necessarily protect us: they protect our ego, our little self. The cost is that they also keep others out. Our hard edges keep us from finding a soft spot for others. Undoing every defense mechanism is not a project for a day or even for a year. But try identifying just *one* hard edge in yourself and try reconditioning yourself a bit. When you feel that edge in a social situation, bring to mind the image of cotton wool and feel yourself yield to your softer, gentler nature.

Exercise for Day Five

Identifying Your Hard Edges

What are your hard edges? What mental, verbal, and physical patterns put a wall between yourself and others? Write just one of these down.

One of my hard edges is:_____

Now close your eyes and envision your mind softening like cotton wool. Experience your own gentleness. Now envision an interaction in which you let go of the pattern and avoid it. How would that go?

Think of a way to put this exercise into practice today with someone you know or love.

Day Six

Integrity

Real integrity is in doing the right thing, knowing that nobody's going to know whether you did it or not.

—Oprah Winfrey

Today's Date: _____

I think most people experience some tension in their lives between the exotic and the practical . . . a life of dreams and a life of realities. For some people, this sets up a dilemma. We long to share the deepest part of ourselves, the part that dares to dream big dreams, the part that trusts deeply in our convictions, the part that aspires to noble and heroic ideals, the part that is the most meaningful to us. But often that deepest part of us is so out of alignment with daily life that we worry about even putting it into words. We feel deep down that we were meant to fulfill an important destiny, that we are here for an important reason, but we cannot see how to get out of the constructed persona, the practical persona, that we have built for ourselves.

Spiritual integrity is the quality of being that prioritizes the transference of dreams into reality, the quality of being that does not settle for less than becoming transparent, honest, and whole now, or at least in the near future. The Latin root *integer* means "whole." To have integrity as a spiritual asset means to be spiritually whole. It means a state of being in which your values move into oneness with your actions, speech, and thoughts. It means living an integral life, not the lives of two people.

Buddhist books are full of great stories about the integrity of sages. Oddly, the quality of integrity is what fills their lives with twists and turns. When you think about it, this makes sense. If a person is really intent on integrating his or her highest values into action, that integration will take priority over an external measure of consistency.

One of my favorite stories is about the great wisdom woman Machig Labdrön, who lived in the eleventh century and founded the Cutting Through (Chöd) lineage in Tibet. Her life started out looking one way and ended up looking quite different, because she was dramatically committed to putting truth—as she understood it at any given time— into action.

As a young woman, Machig was a nun and scholar of the Perfection of Wisdom (Prajnaparamita) Sutra, the most popular religious text of her day. In accord with her monastic vows, she was tidy and disciplined. She rose early in the morning to pray, dressed in clean robes, and kept company with nuns and scholars. She was a model monastic citizen.

One day, she was visited by a lama named Sonam Drakpa. He asked her to explain the Perfection of Wisdom texts to him. She gave him a detailed explanation on the stages of a spiritual practice and on how to reach enlightenment. He commented, "You have a good intellectual understanding of these texts, and you know how to explain them well. However, although you understand the words, you do not really understand the meaning. You have not made the meaning a part of your mind-stream."

"How should I go about this?" she asked, surprised.

"You need to integrate the meaning into your mind. To do that, you have to realize that there is no ultimate difference between subject and object. This is realized through meditative experience, not through book-learning. You must enter nonduality, not just think about it. Thoroughly examine the nature of your mind: all teachings are contained in that."

Machig followed his instructions, examining the nature of her mind. Because she had sharp concentration and her karma was ripe, Lama Sonam's instructions sparked in her a realization, a transcendent awakening experience. Machig had a life-changing epiphany. She realized that the whole spiritual path comes down to cutting through ego-clinging, severing the concepts of "me" and "mine." When ego-clinging is cut, she realized, the walls of duality—the duality of subject and object and the duality of self and other—fall away. She had discovered the Buddhist practice of Chöd, or Cutting Through, a profound and transformative practice that she would devote the rest of her life to propagating.

After this discovery, Machig's life changed almost overnight, as she began putting her discovery of Cutting Through into radical practice. Cutting through attachment to fine clothes, she changed into tattered rags. Cutting off her attachment to place, she left the nunnery and wandered from place to place, like a homeless person. Cutting through attachment to food, she began begging for alms. To stop intellectualizing nonduality, she dropped her studies and left all her books behind. Cutting through attachment to reputation, she began associating with wandering ascetics and lepers who hung out on the fringes of society and in cemeteries. She let her hair grow long and wild. Naturally, people began to talk. What had happened to her? She was such a good nun, so disciplined. Now look at her! She even cut through attachment to her celibate lifestyle and began consorting with a male yogi. Eventually, she became pregnant. With that, she and her husband became the objects of outright gossip. But she ignored it, giving herself to the practice of Cutting Through.

Machig's life reminds us not to live life disconnected from what we value most deeply. We all know people who are disengaged in this way. Many of us live a dual life: the outer life of a constructed self designed to please the conventional world and the inner life of an authentic self—the genius or virtuoso we aspire to become. Some people go on so long with this dual existence that they forget whom it was they were trying to please or what it was they were trying to accomplish in the first place. As the constructed persona becomes a strong habit, the authentic self goes deeper and deeper into the shadows. This creates an unhappy tension in a person's heart.

That person, maybe you, may have forgotten or set aside the dreams of the authentic self, dreamed long ago, perhaps as a child, a teenager, or a college student. When in your life did you feel your authentic self most deeply? When did you become aware of an inner voice that was connecting with outer conditions? When did you feel your calling? When did you feel a sense of purpose? When did you feel you were merging with your best destiny? Remember how you felt, what you yearned for. Did it have a form, or was it indescribable? Where did you imagine it leading you? Did it lead you there? Think back to times—long ago or recent—when you sensed your authentic self surfacing and being nourished. Those memories will provide some good clues as to what it means for you to have spiritual integrity.

Now, as Machig did after her instructions from Lama Sonam, turn your attention to the present and ask the simple question, *To what extent am I living my life right now in harmony with the intentions and aspirations that I value most deeply?* Or you might phrase it, *Am I living my ideal life or only hoping to?* Reflect on that for a minute. It is not necessary or even recommended to change your life radically. The truth is that, for most of us, the instability produced by radical change might not yield the results we hope for. But it is worth experimenting with taking small risks. Consider signing up for a workshop you always wanted to take, kicking a bad habit, learning a skill, planning a retreat, meeting a person who has always inspired you. Seekers have to take risks, or else intentions will just stay in the realm of ideas.

Exercise for Day Six

Taking Small Risks

- Consider: *does my life reflect the values that I hold most deeply?*
- Consider how your life might evolve to be more in harmony with your spiritual journey and with the values you hold dear.
- Write down one small concrete risk you are willing to take this week to bring your life more into harmony with your intention and aspirations.
- Take that small risk.

Day Seven

Self-Inquiry

When I discover who I am, I'll be free.
—Ralph Ellison

Today's Date: _____

*M*achig's profound practice of Cutting Through, as radical as it was for its time, actually builds on a very ancient tradition of self-inquiry. It is a tradition that starts with the question, *Who am I?* Is that not the question of the ages? Theologians, philosophers, sages, scientists—seekers of every sort are fascinated with the question. Even rock stars have asked it. The Buddha's disciples were no exception. They asked the Buddha to weigh in on the existential issue of what constitutes the mysterious "I." He answered the question by pointing to the example of a chariot. A chariot is made up of parts—two wheels, a carriage, seats, and so forth. If you take the chariot apart, is it still a chariot? Not really, because there is no longer one thing. Now there are only the disconnected wheels, carriage, seats, and so forth. You cannot find the actual chariot in any of these parts taken separately. When you put them together, what you have is an assembly of parts. "Chariot" is only a nominal and conceptual designation for those parts that is created in the mind of the observer of the chariot.

Similarly, the Buddha explained, the self is an assembly of parts: a body, consciousness, feelings, perceptions, thoughts. When you deconstruct the body and mind into its parts, it becomes difficult to prove that a self is anything other than a nominal and conceptual designation. Because a self cannot be found, the evidence suggests that the "I" does not truly exist. But it also does not *not* exist! Why? Because there is a conglomeration of parts that functions as a conventional whole. This argument is a very simple explanation of what became the basis for the Buddhist philosophy of *nonself*. But the doctrine of nonself is a subtle and deep philosophy that neither completely denies nor completely affirms the existence of self. A Buddhist might answer the question, "Who are you?" with "*Mu!*" (that is Japanese for "No!"). The question is a non sequitur; it implies the finding of something that cannot be found.

But asking the question is an essential Buddhist practice because, no matter how good we are at philosophical speculation, we all live, breathe, act, speak, and function as if we believed in the existence of a self. To put it in the words of Machig, we still have ego-clinging. We grasp at the idea of "me" and "mine" and construct a whole world around our powerful notion of a self. That would not be so terrible, except that clinging to the notion of a self causes our greatest sufferings and is the single biggest hindrance to developing universal love. It is the barrier that keeps us from recognizing our interdependence with the rest of humanity. Until we actually have an experience of the frailty of our false notion of a self, we will continue to act as if the world revolves around us.

Asking the question, *Who am I?* in the right circumstances (usually in meditation) gives your mind the opportunity to turn inward and experience its own vivid, empty nature that is beyond any conceptual designation. It is possible, over time, through asking this question in a state of deep tranquility, actually to experience the falling away of all the constructions we usually identify with "self" and see through to a deeper reality: selflessness. Put another way, we see through our ego-constructions to a profound, indelible, fundamental ground of being, our true self. As you gradually loosen your habit of grasping at your character traits, body, and thoughts as if they were a solid self, you begin to awaken selfless wisdom and love for all humanity.

In today's exercise, we will look for a self internally to see if we can find it.

Traditional self-searching meditations take a number of forms, but today we will use one of the most concise techniques: turning the mind abruptly inward and asking the question, *Who (or what) is meditating?* One of my meditation teachers described this practice as your eyes looking into your own eyes. A paradox, I know, but paradoxical images are some of the most useful ones to use in meditation. See what happens. Do not harbor a preconceived notion of what you are going to find or not find. Just attempt to look directly at yourself and catch the meditator off guard.

Dharma Tip

This self-inquiry meditation is best done many times over the course of months or years, because what you find, or do not find, may change for you considerably as you get better at this practice and as your general understanding deepens. This is a good practice to carry with you as you move forward on your spiritual journey.

Exercise for Day Seven

Self-Inquiry (Insight) Meditation

- The Three Arrivals: Arrive with body, breath, and mind.
- Say your Awakening Prayer aloud.
- Close your eyes or lower your gaze. Straighten your spine and allow yourself to relax.
- Become aware of the coming and going of breath for several minutes.
- After you are calm, turn your mind's eye inward and abruptly ask, *Who (or what) is meditating?*
- Let everything fall away, and just rest in that, whatever it is.

Day Seven

- When your mind resumes thinking or trying to figure it out, return to the breath for awhile. You can repeat this self-inquiry up to three times during the meditation session. You want to keep the question fresh, your awareness relaxed, and your intuition responsive.
- At the end of the session, say your Dedication Prayer.

May I live in trust, contentment, conscience, and integrity.
May I embrace humanity as my family, appreciate every moment as a gift,
develop spiritual gentleness, and live to serve an altruistic intention.

Service to society is the rent we pay for living on this planet.
—Joseph E. Murray

Week Seven

Grow Your Assets: Self-Discipline, Enthusiasm, Wisdom

Step seven of your spiritual journey is to develop self-discipline, enthusiasm, and wisdom. This week, you will begin to explore the ethical basis for your journey and deepen your understanding of wisdom.

*M*any of my memories of the first few years at the monastery are tied to sitting in the monastery dining room. The dining room was where all the residents gathered three times a day for meals. After the meal prayer—a lengthy intonation if ever there was one!—we would fill our plates and sit at long tables in that big room overlooking the Hudson River. While eating, we watched the barges navigate through ice floes in the winter or carefree sailboats tack upwind in the summer. In the evenings, we watched the sun set as wild turkeys made their way across the long, sloping lawn. This was the hub of social life at the monastery, the one place we all gathered to talk, joke, discuss current construction projects, and share stories.

The abbot of the monastery always sat at the head of one of the tables, and—if there were not many of us in the dining room—I would sometimes have the good luck of being able to sit near him. I remember one of those evenings when, in the course of conversation, someone's name came up, and a person at the table remarked, "Oh, yes, him. He is such a nice person." Suddenly, the abbot exclaimed, "Nice! You people are so funny." (He liked to call us "you people" when he wanted to single us out as Americans.) We all looked at each other, wondering what could strike him as odd about our use of the word *nice*. Then he remarked, "Nice people are everywhere, but *good* people are rare. A good person is straight, not nice. A good person is blunt, not polite."

Day One

Self-Discipline

All faults may be forgiven of him who has perfect candor.
—Thomas Merton

Today's Date: _____

The fifth of Guru Rinpoche's spiritual assets is self-discipline (or *shila* in Sanskrit). Self-discipline was a central part of the Buddha's teaching. Being straight, direct, honest, and transparent are all facets of self-discipline. In the spiritual sense, self-discipline does not just mean self-control. It means appearing to the world the same way you are inwardly: showing up as yourself and staying true to an authenticity from which you speak and act.

To help develop authenticity, the Buddha advised living a principled life. In other words, self-discipline is the art of living life within spiritual boundaries. If a spiritual life were a house, spiritual boundaries would be the walls that contain our practice and that protect us and others from harm.

When our inner teenager hears the word *boundaries* or *rules*, we think, *But I do not want to live by rules! Do not rules mean limitation? How can I become free with more rules? We have enough rules as it is!* Well, I sympathize with the inner teenager . . . we all have her. But on the other hand, consider whether freedom is easier with no boundaries, or within some flexible boundaries. Have you ever tried living with no boundaries? It is an easy way to get into long-term trouble. We need ground rules to provide a good handrail to mark the spiritual path, a reality check when we stray from our intention to serve others. Without personal rules, a search for freedom can inadvertently devolve into a quest for selfish aims.

The tradition of creating temporary rules of self-discipline is tried and true. Catholics have their vows and rituals of fasting. Muslims fast during Ramadan. Jewish people keep dietary and other vows for the Sabbath. Buddhists take one-day vows to refrain from harming others and vows of celibacy. Every religious tradition has its ways of formally enacting spiritual values.

But the truth is, whether we recognize it or not, we already live by rules. Usually these ground rules are set up for us by society and by the law, not by our spiritual conscience. We are socialized into following rules, but we do not often reflect on the underlying themes that bind them together. Great minds, however, even the minds of great politicians like those of this country's founders, did start with themes: preservation of human dignity, peace, and justice, for example. These themes, in our culture and other cultures, not surprisingly, were sometimes inspired by religious traditions, which acted as the moral (and sometimes political) fabric of society.

If our goal is to serve, respect, and care for the family of living beings, we would at the very least have to live a life that refrains from harm. But how? Is there a recipe for actions that guide us in that direction? The Buddha came up with such a recipe. He outlined ten general moral imperatives that help us imagine what a life of avoiding harm would look like when translated into our actions, speech, and thoughts.

The Buddha's ten moral imperatives help us accomplish two very simple and important goals: to be straight (that is, straightforward, honest, and nondeceptive) and to be kind. This first goal helps us avoid harming others. The second goal helps us aid others, respect them, and love them better. These two goals are two sides of the same coin. If we are going to serve humanity, we need to find our freedom within boundaries. We need to recognize that the liberty we seek is sought for every single living creature, so every action we engage in should reflect communal consciousness. However, we also need to melt the boundaries that prevent us from feeling with the world. For this, we need some guidelines that encourage us to take the empathetic, rather than the selfish, perspective.

Day One

What did the Buddha recommend?

1. Practice nonviolence. To be on a spiritual path, we need—first and foremost—to respect life and act to preserve it. Life is sacred.

2. Respect property. Property is what belongs to others or the community at large. It is an extension of humanity and even of life itself. Pilfering, borrowing without asking, or taking what is not given are all contrary to respecting property. More broadly, respecting property means not being stealthy or deceitful with your actions.

3. Be sexually responsible. To avoid harming others with your sexuality, design specific commitments of sexual responsibility that work for you and stick to them. Your sexuality is a vehicle for your devotion to humanity. If you are in a relationship, keep your agreements and commitments, spoken and unspoken. Use your sexuality to strengthen your relationships rather than to tear them apart.

4. Be honest and direct. To live a good life, we should develop good speech. It is worth developing a strong habit of being straight and telling the truth, even when it is hard to do. If you do not develop the habit of honesty, people will lose trust in you. If they lose trust in you, your opportunity to be a light and a refuge to others will be deeply impaired. So honesty is extremely important.

5. Speak with kindness. Speak gently to others, as if you were speaking to your parent, to a child, or to a good friend. How we speak can do wonders for how we come across to others. If you consider yourself a naturally rough type, do not think your speech is beyond gentling! Speaking kindly is a skill. It does not mean being withdrawn or flat. You can be boisterous, outspoken, and kind at the same time.

6. Make peace (help mediate between divided parties). When it comes to arguments or quarrels, skillful intervention can be a blessing. Assess the situation. If you think you can help, do not stand by in idleness. See if you can find a way to defuse negative feelings and bring divided parties to a common ground. Instead of running from discord, use the opportunity to sharpen your peacemaking skills.

7. Speak meaningfully. Speech is our mode of communicating love and truth. To use it well, be mindful of the content of your speech instead of resorting to habit. Does what you say reflect what you really believe? Is it helpful to this listener in this context? Are you making a deeper connection with the listener or just speaking aimlessly?

8. Be loving and forgiving in spirit. We become what we think about. If you are going to develop universal love, begin with loving thoughts. Work to deepen the sense of warmth that you have for others from moment to moment. Forgive them their mistakes and look on each one as an only child.

9. Be generous of heart. To live a spiritual life, you need to give up jealousy and covetousness, since these sentiments interfere with being magnanimous. Make generosity a frame of mind. Instead of coveting what others have, rejoice that they have it.

10. Keep your perspective in line with truth. Plumbing the depths of truth is a lifelong endeavor. Keep your view in line with your deeper insights. Let truth really seep into your day-to-day life, not just bounce off you.

When I first heard these moral imperatives, I had a sense of relief. Finally, some simple guidelines that are in line with spiritual life! At the time, I was in India studying in the birthplace of the Buddha, Bodh Gaya. I copied the list in my best handwriting, with a calligraphy pen, in Tibetan script and English, on my toughest paper (living in Asia is notoriously hard on everything flimsy) and memorized it. In the hazy Indian heat, I recited it over to myself every day for a month until I could recall each one by heart.

Day One

The Buddha's moral imperatives seem simple, but they are deceptively profound. In my own life, I come back to them again and again. Nothing has been a better touchstone when I am having trouble knowing what the right thing to do might be. And when I stray off the path, it is these guidelines that remind me of where I took a wrong turn. It may sound old fashioned, but sometimes the traditional recipes are still the most tried and true.

Ten imperatives are a lot to focus on at once, so today, pick three of the Buddha's moral imperatives and use them to generate questions. You should pick three imperatives that challenge you to think more deeply about your own values and behavior. For example, your list might read:

Respect property (the Buddha's second moral imperative). Do I respect the property of others? Do I use what belongs to others or to my community carelessly, without permission or without being thankful for its use? What are the consequences of my behavior toward others' property, toward the communal property of the planet? What would happen if I started respecting the property of my neighbors, family, friends, community? What would that look like for me in action?

Be honest and direct (the Buddha's fourth moral imperative). Am I honest, direct, transparent? In what ways do I avoid being honest with my speech? In what situations? For what reasons? What are the short- and long-term consequences of being honest and direct? Of being dishonest or indirect? What would my life be like if I always told the truth? How would that serve others? What would that look like for me in action?

Be loving in spirit (the Buddha's eighth moral imperative). Am I always loving? In what situations do my patience and warmth deteriorate? Is it possible to be loving and irritated at the same time? How can I become more loving in spirit?

Now consider what moral imperatives you would design to help you steer your life in a better direction. What would you do specifically to become more straight with others and more loving toward them?

When I first tried this exercise, I thought, *Oh, no problem! I am honest and direct. I am nonviolent. I do not participate in killing. I do most of these things anyway.* But then I began to think more deeply. The deeper I thought, the more I realized that while I did not exactly flaunt these moral imperatives, I did not really live by them, either. For example, I did not catch myself lying very often, but in many situations I avoided being transparent, sometimes just from force of habit. While I thought of myself as nonviolent, did I not sometimes act aggressively? While I thought of myself as loving, did I not sometimes get irritable and impatient? Being straight is harder than we think!

Today, you will select or design three moral imperatives. While you are carrying these moral imperative with you, see what you find out about yourself and what you notice. The point is not to judge yourself or feel bad about your actions. The point of the exercise is to notice and evaluate your actions, in relation to the values that you hold dear. This is an exercise to see what it is like to hold to some firm ethical principles. The point is to begin to design the contours of an ethical life.

We can enjoy the benefits of this practice by picking a principle— nonviolence, for example—and then really living by it for a day, a few days, or a week. Just doing something like this for a day or two can be very revealing. It is like a reality test of where we live ethically and spiritually.

When you are developing self-discipline, begin with small steps. Identify one area where you wish to be more straight, more disciplined, more confident. Then create a few small resolutions to keep for just a couple of days. For example, you might make truth-telling your goal. Then you would create this resolution: *For the next three days, I will tell the truth. I will be honest with everyone around me.* Or you might want to renounce a bad habit, say, watching too much television. You might make the resolution, *I will watch only X minutes of TV for the next three days.* If you are inspired to extend your resolutions, making them an integral part of your life, you can do so.

Making a resolution differs from making intentions and aspirations. A resolution is a personal commitment to take action. Taking spiritual vows or making resolutions is an ancient practice spanning all religious traditions. It is a powerful method for cultivating an ethical basis for the rest of your life.

Exercise for Day One:

Finding Your Bottom Line

Consider: *What do I really believe is right? What do I know is wrong?*

Using this reflection as a basis, write three moral imperatives you can observe for the rest of this week. You can use some of the Buddha's imperatives or design your own.

Write down your three moral imperatives here:

1. _____

2. _____

3. _____

Read these over at the end of each day and reflect on each one. For each one, ask the questions, *Did I observe this moral imperative today? In what ways did I stray, or keep to it? In what ways can I deepen and go further with this moral imperative tomorrow?*

Day Two

Enthusiasm

The restless, agitated mind,
Hard to protect, hard to control,
The sage makes it straight,
As a fletcher the shaft of an arrow.

—The Buddha

Today's Date: _____

What are you truly passionate about? What makes you lose track of time? What gives you joy while also building your self-esteem? Everyone has had something about which they felt enthusiastic or passionate at some time in their life. You undoubtedly already have a taste of what enthusiasm feels like. But certainly not one of us is enthusiastic about everything all the time. How many people do you know who are enthusiastic about most parts of their life? Those people are more the exception than the rule, but we do occasionally run into them.

I had an Uncle Jess who was such a person. Good old Uncle Jess was a logger in Idaho, rough around the edges, bawdy in the joke department, and one of those people who loved his job, loved his wife, loved his life, and had a sense of humor about everything else. You probably know someone like that. Are these people charmed? Not likely. If you really look into it, you will discover that these exceptional people are all privy to a secret: passion is a cultivated art.

When I first began practicing Buddhism in earnest at the monastery, I asked my teacher what I should do in the way of spiritual practice. Where should I start? Which practice should I make my priority? The lama suggested that I start a set of practices called *ngondro*, which means

Day Two

"preliminary practices." These practices prepare students for some of the more involved meditations in the Tibetan Buddhist path. The first part of ngondro involves doing one hundred thousand prostrations, laying yourself full out on the ground one hundred thousand times. It is a bit like an extended marathon that tends to take weeks, months, or years, depending on how many you do every day.

I dove right into this practice. It took me about six months to complete. I would start after breakfast every day and prostrate before a statue of the Buddha until lunchtime. Then I would take a midday break. I would begin again at about three and go until five. In this way, I passed months. In truth, I was very enthusiastic about the practice, but it was certainly physically challenging. It taught me that I could do more than I thought possible in a day. It taught me that boundaries can be pushed. After completing that practice, I was told that the next part involved the recitation of one hundred thousand long mantras. Things continued in this way for many more months. Eventually, in about two years, I finished all the preliminary practices. I was elated! Finally the pain was over! Certainly after all this, the lama would give me some kind of profound practice or meditation. There must be some kind of amazing reward to look forward to after such a monumental effort, after thousands of hours of difficult practices.

I imagined that he would give me instructions on one of the advanced practices that I had heard about in my time at the monastery, one of the secret meditations that quicken the path to enlightenment. I was full of anticipation when I went up to Lama's little room to tell him the good news: I had finished the hundreds of thousands of repetitions of prostrations and mantras and prayers. Lama simply said, "That is very good. You should do it again."

"Again?" I asked tentatively. "Um, isn't there something else?"

He did not suggest anything else. Instead, he mused, "I think it would be very good if you do it all again." I was speechless. Surely he did not mean for me to repeat the preliminary practices all over again? But, as I ascertained after further inquiry, that is exactly what he meant. Of course, I was stunned. It had taken a lot of perseverance and pushing

249

through my laziness to complete the first set of preliminary practices. Thousands of hours. Sore muscles, painful joints, boredom. I could not imagine doing it again.

Later I brought my dejection to Lama. I felt discouraged. He laughed. When Lama laughs, his eyes turn up in a way that is simply contagious. You cannot help but smile. I remember the laugh . . . it had a certain good-humored compassion in it. It said, without him having to say it, "You still have a lot to learn about what this path is about."

But he just said, "Did you know the Buddha taught that discouragement is just a form of laziness?" I think it was with that comment that a trickle of understanding began to seep through the wall of my disheartenment. Lama had placed the responsibility for feeling downtrodden and overwhelmed right in my lap. It seemed to me that external conditions were responsible for my discouragement. Is not the downtrodden person justified in finally giving up? That is what I had always believed. But here the responsibility was being placed squarely on me. *Discouragement*, I repeated to myself, *is a form of laziness.* It became my mantra when I woke up the next morning. It became the phrase that got me into the shrineroom to begin the preliminary practices yet again and to continue every day for the next two years in the repetition of, yet again, one hundred thousand prostrations.

Dharma Tip

Enthusiasm takes energy. When you feel as if you do not have the energy to be enthusiastic, consider one inherent source of energy at your disposal: emotional energy. Even depression, a state that many people consider lethargic, is often a manifestation of repressed emotional energy. If you can get in touch with that underlying emotional energy, it is possible to channel it into enthusiasm for your passion, your spiritual journey, your everyday dharma, and perseverance to see your path through to its completion.

Day Two

Over time, I learned that underlying Lama's advice was an even more profound concept: perseverance feeds passion, and the other way around. We are not automatically overjoyed and enthusiastic about serving humanity. It will mean a lot of inconvenience to our ego. It will mean hardship. We will get bored and bedraggled and discouraged. We will get tired. To counteract our tendency to get discouraged and give up, we need to work on two levels.

First, we need to reflect frequently on the big picture. Is there any more exciting picture than the journey as we have imagined it?

Second, we have to be creative: we have to create diligence and enthusiasm. We must *already* have diligence and enthusiasm in place. Diligence is a no-nonsense attitude, and enthusiasm is an optimistic energy. The remarkable thing is that joy and enthusiasm can and must be cultivated for us really to accomplish anything in life, not to mention the amazing project of serving humanity. And another remarkable thing is that enthusiasm and perseverance fuel each other. No one is going to serve you enthusiasm on a silver platter. What's more, when your enthusiasm wanes, you cannot count on anyone but yourself to rekindle it.

When you get into a groove of rekindling enthusiasm daily, it becomes easier to persevere, to follow through to the end. For me, completing the preliminary practices the second time became a study in joy, enthusiasm, and follow-through. I was doing something that I did not particularly want to do. But, by God (or by Buddha), I was going to do it and do it well. With this attitude, I started to understand the term *spiritual warrior*. I went to war with my laziness, to war with my discouragement. I convinced myself not to lose this battle. For me, the point of this practice was to work with my resistance.

I think battling laziness and complacency is one of the key points to spiritual practice. You begin by simply pushing yourself beyond where you thought you could go. Limits are largely self-created. Enthusiasm is best cultivated by not making things harder for yourself than they actually are.

Exercise for Day Two

Working with Discouragement

What do you feel discouraged about in your life? In what ways you are not living up to your own expectations? Pick one very specific area where you feel as if you have fallen short of your ideal for yourself and write this down here:

I am discouraged about _____

_____

Now write down three reasons you feel that you are falling short (e.g., *I cannot do it; I am not talented enough; I do not have time*):

1. _____

2. _____

3. _____

What would it mean if you were to reframe these reasons? What if the reasons you give for failure were reframed as a form of particular laziness? Particular laziness means you might be lazy in one area but not in others. How would that affect how you come at the problem?

If solving the problem really were as simple as getting up and doing something, what specific activities or steps would you take (keep these very small, specific, and action oriented) to counteract your old patterns?

Day Two

I will take the following small, specific actions this week to counteract this particular laziness:

1. _____

2. _____

3. _____

Day Three

The Three C's of Enthusiasm

Live as if you were to die tomorrow. Learn as if you were to live forever.

—Gandhi

Today's Date: _____

$\mathcal{F}$inding passion and overcoming laziness go a long way to kindle and sustain enthusiasm for the spiritual journey. But there are also a number of other qualities that support enthusiasm. Some of the most important are curiosity, carefulness, and concentration: I call these "the three C's."

Curiosity. To feed enthusiasm for your spiritual life, you need to keep learning, to be insatiably curious about the world. One of the modern embodiments of this kind of curiosity is His Holiness the 14th Dalai Lama. From the time he was a young boy, he was fascinated by how things work and—even in the far away, isolated kingdom of Tibet—used to take apart (and put back together) engines and clocks in his spare time. Now, many decades later, he meets annually with a group of scientists to engage in spiritual-secular dialogue about issues that concern both the scientific and the Buddhist communities. He is one of very few traditional Buddhist leaders to be so deeply interested in science.

In one sutra, it says that a buddha's wisdom is like the ocean, both vast and deep. As long as you remain curious, you will reach out to know things both broadly and deeply. The more deeply you know something, the closer you come to wisdom. The more broadly you know something, the better you will be able to apply that wisdom skillfully for the benefit of others. One of the great masters of the nineteenth century, Jamgon Kongtrul, advised his students to read widely, not limiting themselves to the writings of one sect or viewpoint. If you read many viewpoints, he advised, one of them will eventually open up your wisdom and push your understanding deeper. So be diligent about learning.

One common question I get at meditation retreats is, "Is it okay to be a spiritual dabbler?" Well, there is not one right answer. I personally believe a lot can be gained by initially studying widely, investigating various paths and teachers. In the spiritual smorgasbord that is America, that is an easy task. Even if you do not have money, if you are resourceful, you can make contact with a number of traditions, starting on the Internet. There are, without a doubt, spiritual centers locally. Check them out, and also check around them. Google them. Are there scandals there, problems? Attend some meetings, meet some people. But be circumspect—investigate with a number of questions in your back pocket.

Then, once you find a spiritual path that feels right, spend a long time around it. If there is a teacher or teachers, spend months, even years, around that person before making commitments. But once you feel comfortable and are finding what you hunger for, begin to go deep with those practices. At that point, stop dabbling and delve into a tradition or mode of practice. If you do not go deep, you will become a mere spiritual window shopper, or a retreat junkie. You will have a lot of fun experiences, but you may return from your buffet hungry. Or when times get rough, you will not have a sound spiritual foundation on which to rest. So my general advice to students with regard to spiritual practice is to start wide and end deep.

Carefulness. The greater care you take in the midst of action, the better the quality of your work. The better your work, the easier it is to sustain enthusiasm. So when you undertake something, do it thoroughly, do it well, do it with care.

On my first trip to eastern Tibet, I visited a place called Korche Monastery. One of my teachers was sponsoring the rebuilding of the monastery, which had been flattened by bombs during the Chinese invasion of Tibet in 1959. I had the good fortune to be able to watch a couple of thanka painters work on some fine statues and murals. I watched them quite a bit, because the days in Tibet are long and there is not much to do—no radio, no TV, no distractions. The painters were both young monks in training to become specialized artists, and they were taking great care with their work. I noticed that to complete just a single face on one statue would take each of them a day. At this rate, it would take them many months to complete this project. I asked one of them how the system works. Did he work under contract? Did he get anything for all these hours of work?

"Get?" He smiled kindly, then laughed. "I get more patient! This is what I do. I am an artist."

In time, this monk became a good friend. He has become a fine thanka and mural painter. He paints as an offering and because it is his spiritual practice. He recently finished painting the inside of a large Tibetan stupa in New York. His room and board was supplied by the monastery, but he expected no payment in return for his work. He also expected no recognition, no showings, no purchases of his work. As is Tibetan custom, he does not sign his name to anything. He sees his reward in terms of spiritual assets. Patience is one, but others are thoroughness, carefulness, and an ability to follow any project through to its end. Being careful and thorough is its own reward.

Concentration. When you are fully concentrated, any activity can be meditation. Concentration is a bit like a cerebral muscle. The more you hold your attention to something without distraction, the stronger the muscle gets. When I first moved into the monastery, I discovered quickly that Buddhist monks and nuns engage in concentration practices that are not always identified as such explicitly. One of the best is liturgical chanting.

Have you ever followed along with a song sheet or a hymn book to a song that you do not know well? To keep up, you have to sustain a certain level of concentration. Well, imagine doing that for hours and in a different language. That is what a native Buddhist religious chanting session is like. If you have ever been a Gregorian monk, you might know. The process of learning to chant liturgies in Tibetan is an amazing practice for developing concentration and focus. This was a surprise to me. When I first sat down to one of these sessions, I thought it might be about prayer or about visualization or meditation. But if you are not a very fast reader in Tibetan (and I was not), it becomes all about concentration, about simply reading the words, and then eventually about letting sounds come out of your mouth in time with the other chanters.

I learned that concentration really is a muscle and that there is a balance between concentrating too hard and not hard enough. If you are concentrating too hard, you lose the flow of the chanting. If you do not concentrate hard enough, you get distracted. So I worked on balance. The concentration required to chant takes sustained effort. At first there is a process of dragging your mind back again and again to the words. As you get better, your mind stays on them for longer and longer. Eventually, you become absorbed in the process and begin to lose yourself. You get into that mystical zone.

I sometimes teach Buddhist practices to my students that require chanting in Tibetan. I encourage them to discover the hidden benefits of chanting, because they are not necessarily obvious to a beginner. One of the hidden benefits is the development of balanced concentration. This benefit can actually come from any activity: we perform tasks every day—driving, mowing the lawn, eating, washing dishes—that hold the potential for developing relaxed, single-pointed concentration. Try sustaining your attention more mindfully the next time you do a small task that is usually automatic. Pretend you are doing it for the first time.

From the point of view of Buddhist meditation, and from the point of view of many Buddhist art forms, activity without concentration is activity unfulfilled. For a person who has not experienced concentration, it is hard to explain its benefits. Concentration is necessary in painting, in dancing, and especially in meditation. The kind of meditation in which concentration is consciously induced is called *shinay* (or *shamatha* or "mindfulness") meditation. The meditator focuses the mind on a real or visualized object without wavering. At first, of course, the mind will not stay on the object. The meditator must bring the mind back again and again to the object of focus.

The phrase used to describe this beginner's mind is "monkey mind." The mind bounces about, unable to rest on one thing for very long. But concentration is like a muscle. It can be trained and built up. The first way to train the mind is to use a faculty called "mindfulness," which is like a tether that anchors attention to the object. So, for example, let us suppose you want to use an object that you have in front of you—the edge of a table, or a pattern on your bedspread—as your focus. Take a minute and put aside this book and focus your attention on something without wavering. Become absorbed simply in the experience of perceiving that object. Without becoming involved in thoughts about the object, just rest your attention simply and nondistractedly on it. What does that feel like? It is not uncommon to experience such a moment as fresh and new, as if you have just been born in this moment.

Exercise for Day Three

Concentration Meditation

- Place a natural object in front of you.
- Rest your gaze on the object while relaxing the mind.
- Practice just being present with the object without trying to identify it, label it, or note its characteristics.
- Practice being nondistracted.

Day Three

- When your mind wanders, gently return your attention to the object.
- Keep your concentration relaxed but focused.
- After about five minutes of focusing, rest your mind.
- Finish your meditation with a dedication.

Day Four

Wisdom

Words of truth are always paradoxical.
—Lao Tzu

Today's Date: _____

The final asset, the pinnacle of all the others, is wisdom. We will be spending the next three days on it. Wisdom, in Buddhism, does not refer only to kitchen-table wisdom. It refers to that part of our mind that knows truth—not partial truths, but the whole truth. Nothing can be said about truth. You might think I am kidding, but I am not. As soon as you try to put truth into words, it is no longer truth itself; it is just an approximation. Any expression of what is "real" veers off from truth itself. Why? The answer is that truth is nondualistic. Language, however, lives in the world of duality, of subject/object and self/other. That is why truth cannot be communicated in words. It can be understood only through insight—it can be communicated only from you to you.

No story illustrates this more vividly, perhaps, than a scene in the story of Vimalakirti. Vimalakirti was a layman who has been something of an inspiration to generations of Buddhists. The Sutra of Vimalakirti all takes place in Vimalakirti's house, where he is convalescing from an illness. A few disciples of the Buddha drop by to visit him because they have heard of his great wisdom. They come to discuss with him spiritual and philosophical questions. At one point, the conversation turns to the nondual nature of wisdom. Each bodhisattva, standing around Vimalakirti's bed, eloquently expresses his personal understanding of nonduality. Then Manjushri, who is acting as a moderator, turns to Vimalakirti for the last word. Vimalakirti, they are all starting to suspect, is the wisest man in the room. The room falls silent. Manjushri says, "We have all given our teachings. You, Vimalakirti, are the last among us, and the wisest. Tell us: How should we understand the truth of nonduality?"

In response, Vimalakirti says nothing at all. This moment is sometimes referred to in Buddhist texts as "Vimalakirti's thunderous silence." It so moved and stimulated the other disciples in the room that many of them awakened on the spot. They congratulated him for indeed having given the most profound teaching.

Why did Vimalakirti say nothing? As soon as we try to analyze Vimalakirti's pure silence, we may do it some disservice. So my apologies, Vimalakirti. He will, I hope, understand, in his ineffable wisdom, why I try to explain. We have to start somewhere! Vimalakirti was demonstrating that truth cannot be analyzed. It cannot be broken down into language and descriptions. It can only be understood through the nondual wisdom in which the knower and that which is known are nondifferentiable.

How can the knower and the known be nondifferentiable? They become nondifferentiable when the knower (that means you) loses the idea of "self" and "other." Some semblance of this happens to us occasionally even in our ordinary state. Have you ever been so deeply involved in something that you become a part of it? This experience is what is sometimes popularly referred to as "being in the zone." Activities that my friends and students have cited in which they lost themselves include golf, baseball, sewing, calligraphy, and painting. Any activity that involves mindfulness or concentration, or else a sense of letting-go, can put you close to a nondual experience.

You might wonder if enlightenment can be achieved this way. Can insight be acquired through menial tasks such as sewing and doing dishes? The answer is most definitely yes. In ancient India, the Buddhist tradition tell us, there were eighty-four great meditation masters, called the Eighty-four Mahasiddhas. You might think that, being meditation masters, they must have been cave-dwelling ascetics, monks, or kings with the leisure to devote their lives to meditation. Not so. They were tailors, shoemakers, housewives, prostitutes, beer-sellers, farmers, cooks, fishermen, butchers, and so on. One of these great masters, Tilopa, attained enlightenment by grinding sesame seeds. He took his job as an analogy for the spiritual path: he compared the seeds to the mind, his grinding to meditation, and the oil he pressed out to the wisdom-nature. He ground his way to enlightenment.

Nondual activity is something that you can train in. It is what meditators work to accomplish in meditation, but a cushion is not required. The best activities with which to attempt this are those that do not involve using your discursive mind much: short, simple activities, not brain-teasers. Repetitive tasks that involve some concentration, like sewing, doing yoga, jogging, or peeling apples, are good. Find a task to practice with. Start your task. When you are somewhat into it, see if you can become fully immersed in the activity until you become one with it and lose yourself. Allow yourself—your whole body, breath, and attention—to become one with your movement, so that there is no differentiation between you and your activity. When you do this, you will have a moment where you have a reduced sense of self—a moment in which you become your activity. This is a moment of nonduality, where the separation between subject and object, the separation between you and the world, narrows or even disappears. This moment reveals the dharma present in everyday actions.

Exercise for Day Four

Hidden Wisdom in Everyday Actions

- Choose a simple, repetitive activity.
- While you are involved in this activity, see how absorbed you can become in it.

- Release your sense of self. See if you can become one with your activity and wash dishes without a washer, sew without a sewer, and so on. What is it like to be the activity?
- Finish your activity with a dedication.

Day Five

Wisdom as Innate

In each and every living being, the Real exists—waiting to be realized.

—Saraha

Today's Date: _____

From the perspective of the ancient wisdom traditions, wisdom is ultimately not acquired or developed, created or fashioned: it is innate. It is innate in the sense that it not constructed; you do not have to "try" to have wisdom. It is also innate in the sense that wisdom is born with you. It permeates every experience, even the experiences you are having right now. You are already wise—you just have yet to realize it.

How could we already be wise? We do not feel wise. True, you do not feel your own wisdom. If you did, it would be an object of feeling. But wisdom is not an object of feeling. It is not an object at all. It has no shape, no color, no fixed location. You cannot touch it. You cannot even conceive of it. If you could, it would not be *of* you; it would be an object of your attention or intellect. It would be something you reflect on, not something that is the very essence of your being. Innate wisdom is more than an idea: it exists within and of you. It is too intimate to be known with mind, because it is the mind, in its quintessential sense. Wisdom is awareness, the bare, naked, aware, conscious nature of mind. In the Buddhist tradition, it is called innate, reflexive, or organic awareness.

Organic awareness simply refers to the natural, ever-present, aware quality of your experience from moment to moment. Right now, you are aware. You are awake and conscious. That awakeness, that consciousness, in the most simple and essential sense, is organic to you. It is an integral part of you.

Ultimately, wisdom *is* awareness. Or put another way, the nature of awareness is wisdom. As you may already suspect, this idea links awareness, in and of itself, to the idea of buddha-nature, or wisdom-nature. Discovering your wisdom-nature means coming face to face with the nature of your awareness. It does not mean embracing the objects of your awareness as wisdom; it means embracing the awareness *itself* as wisdom.

To do this, we must distinguish between the mind's *expression* and its *essence*. Mind is not the only thing with an expression and an essence. Each and every thing has an expression, but it also has something deeper and more pervasive—an essential nature. This nature goes beyond expression. There are a number of ways to understand the difference between expression and essence. Take water as an example. I like this example, because everyone—in every country and community—knows what water is. Water does not just have one expression. It takes many forms. When water takes the form of a lake, it might be blue, on a clear day. But then the weather changes, and the water is gray. Or the sun sets, and all those colors are reflected in the lake. Clearly, the water's expression—its visual quality—changes with time and circumstances.

But there are qualities of water that do not change over time. Wetness, for example. Wetness is an inherent, essential quality of water. No matter how it appears, water is always wet. When it is frozen, it is not wet, but then it is also no longer technically water: it is ice. Wetness and liquidity define water, just as heat defines fire and changeableness defines clouds. Wetness is water's "essence." Wetness is organic to water.

In the same way, the mind has an *expression* and an *essence*. The expressions of the mind are thoughts, emotions, feelings, concepts, perceptions. These—like the changing qualities of water—are temporarily present, but they are not the essence of the mind. How do we know that thoughts and so forth are not an essential part of mind? One reason we know this is because there are times when we are not thinking—for example, when in a deep state of sleep. There are times when we are not feeling, and so forth.

Is there anything that is with us at *all* times, that never leaves us? There is. Like water and wetness, the mind also has an unchanging nature, an essence, that never departs from the mind. That essence is awareness. While the content of our thoughts changes, and our emotions change, awareness permeates every moment of waking experience. It is the soil out of which every experience is made. It is organic to the mind. Like the wetness of water, awareness defines the mind, no matter what its expression.

So the primary goal of a meditator is gradually to come to know the nature, or essence, of his or her own mind—awareness—first through recognizing its qualities and then through a more natural process of instant recognition. The process is a little like learning to recognize a face in a crowd. The face of the person has been described to you, but you have never met her. At first, you must look for the characteristics of the person—you have been told she has black hair and dark eyes and is wearing a green sweater. So you look until you notice someone like that. Once you have found her, you can recognize her quickly, and you no longer have to think, *black hair, dark eyes, green sweater*. You know her face in an instant. The same goes for the nature of awareness. At first, you become acquainted with its qualities, and then you begin to recognize awareness for yourself. Once you have seen it, you no longer need to focus on its qualities separately, just as you would not need consciously to look for the traits of a good friend in order to recognize her. You just know her. In that way, you come to know awareness as your own true face.

Day Five

Exercise for Day Five
Meditation on the Essence

- Practice the Three Arrivals.
- Begin your meditation with your Awakening Prayer.
- After a few minutes of resting the mind, notice the panorama of your mental experience. Notice how thoughts, feelings, and sensory experiences arise and dissolve. These are the mind's expressions.
- Now focus on one particular thought or feeling. Try resting in the essence of that thought but not in its form, its content, or its details. Instead, rest in the ground from which it seems to arise and into which it seems to dissolve.
- What is that experience like? If you find yourself letting go of all reference points, just let that process occur and stay in it as long as possible.
- Finish your meditation with your Dedication Prayer.

Day Six

Three Qualities of Awareness

The art of being wise is the art of knowing what to overlook.
—William James

Today's Date: _____

O rganic awareness is simply the knower of all things, the experiencer. Without awareness, you could not read the words on this page. Awareness is the most fundamental quality of knowing, before there is a sense of a self that knows. Awareness is the simple moment of knowing without a knower—thinking without a thinker—perceiving without a perceiver—experiencing without an experiencer. Awareness is the "you" before the labels of name, personality, and habits, for example. The wisdom-nature has a core, a most fundamental element, and awareness is it.

Awareness, while an extremely subtle quality of our being, is also pervasive. For that reason, while it is hard to grasp, it is very present to us, somewhat like space. Since it is present, it can be recognized by a persistent meditator. It can be recognized because we *experience* it. We experience the qualities of awareness, even when we may not yet recognize them. Through noticing these qualities, awareness comes slowly into focus as a recognizable element of our experience.

Awareness has three qualities. These qualities are simple. They are subtle. They permeate every experience—our most depressing ones, our happiest ones, and everything in between. These qualities are luminosity, emptiness, and unimpededness.

Luminosity. What does it mean to say that awareness is luminous? It does not mean that awareness is glowing with some kind of physical light or that we can expect some kind of flash of light when we see awareness. Awareness is simply and naturally a light unto itself. It has its own life, its own vividness, its own energy, its own knowing quality. That is what is meant by luminosity. While experiences change, the light-unto-itself quality of the mind does not. You can check this yourself and see if it is the case. Is your mind, your awareness, self-luminous? Try asking yourself this question when your eyes are open. Is this awareness dark and solid, or is it vivid and clear? Now close your eyes. Is there a quality of consciousness present—a *knower*? Is that knower dark and solid, or is there a constant, clear, luminous, vivid aspect to that knower? Look at your own experience, your own mental reality in this moment, and see.

Emptiness. Does awareness have the quality of emptiness? Does awareness exist? It would not make sense to say, "No, it does not exist at all," because we can empirically verify that we are aware. Our experience does not have the quality of a vacuum. To say that awareness has the quality of emptiness means that, while awareness is luminous, it is not a thing. It has no inherent identity: nothing you can point to and say, "This is it!" It has no shape, color, location, or size. It is free from solidity. It is not empty in the sense of an empty vase or an empty cup, containing nothing at all. It is empty in the sense of being free from an identity. It goes beyond expression and language; it is beyond the grasp of a dualistic mind. In this sense, it is empty.

One way to understand the empty quality of awareness through your own experience is to notice that awareness is inherently spacious. Without even thinking about awareness per se, notice the quality of your experience right now. Your mind provides the field of observation. Within your experience, your momentary conscious experience now, there is a quality of dimensionality. Your experience is not flat. There is a space in which all kinds of thoughts and appearances unfold within dimensionality: a space of mind. While there is a colorful and dynamic aspect to experience and to sense perception—while there is a dramatic play of experience, so to speak—there is also a stage or a canvas, an underlying space in which all this occurs. When we are in the audience watching a play, we pay attention to the players and to the action of the drama. We rarely pay attention to the stage itself. In the same way, our mind is full of its own dramas. Engrossed in these dramas, we rarely pay attention to the space of the mind. The stage or canvas is this space, a space so subtle we do not see it unless it is pointed out. This space is the emptiness of awareness.

Unimpededness. This luminous, empty awareness has one other quality: it is unimpeded. To say awareness is unimpeded means that awareness is without limits or without an edge. Try to find an edge to your awareness. Is there a place beyond which you cannot be aware, *within* the quality of your experience? You might say, *I cannot know what is occurring outside my mind—for example, in the mind of someone else*. But that is not looking at the quality of your experience. That is imagining *something else* outside your mind's experience. It is not looking directly at the field of what you know. If you look directly at the field of your experience, if you close your eyes and just notice the awareness, the knower, the experiencer—you cannot find a single part of your own experience that is not pervaded by that knower. Awareness is everywhere. It has no constraints or borders. This is also true with respect to time. Awareness is unstoppable. It follows you from moment to moment. In the sense of both space and time, awareness is unimpeded.

There is a final point about these qualities that is important to note. Luminosity, emptiness, and unimpededness are inseparable. It is not that awareness is sometimes luminous, sometimes empty, and sometimes unimpeded. It is always all three. We, however, may be paying attention to one of these qualities at the expense of the others. In the beginning, your examination will have to be one-sided, just as you would look for a green sweater in a crowd before you know the person you are looking for. But awareness itself is not any one of these qualities alone; it is the inseparability of all three qualities. Awareness is luminous, empty, and unimpeded all at the same time. Awareness is, to put it another way, the very embodiment of deepest wisdom: self-illuminating, nondual, and without limit. That is why the great sages remind us again and again: aside from the mind, there is no other buddha.

Exercise for Day Six

Meditation on Luminosity, Emptiness, and Unimpededness

- Practice the Three Arrivals.
- Begin your meditation with your Awakening Prayer.
- As you did in yesterday's meditation, notice the panorama of your mental experience. As you investigate the following questions, give yourself plenty of time to explore and rest in what you find.
- Now ask yourself if there is a luminous quality to this experience. Is it dull, or is the mind pervaded by a bright quality of knowing? Give yourself some time to look into this and rest with what you find.
- After a few minutes, ask yourself whether this mental experience is one-dimensional or whether there is a spacious quality to it. Is there a space in which all these thoughts unfold? Rest in that for a few minutes.
- Finally, ask yourself if there is a limit or edge to your awareness. Is awareness infinite? Rest in what you find.
- Finish your meditation with your Dedication Prayer.

Day Seven

Processing the Journey

An unanswered question is a fine traveling companion. It sharpens your eye for the road.

—Rachel Naomi Remen

Today's Date: _____

One of the defining characteristics of a bodhisattva, a sage in the Buddhist tradition, is that she intentionally postpones her enlightenment in order to remain in the world. She wants to live in relationship with others, to be reachable, to stay human. A subtext of this characteristic is that—for a seeker whose heart is in the right place—the spiritual path is never about the destination. It is not about the thought, *I want to be enlightened.* It is about the process. It is about the journey. Dharma is not a solitary quest for wisdom or nirvana—it is a communal vision of what is possible here on earth.

On this final day of your seven-week odyssey, how does it feel looking back? What practices have been most doable, the most transformative? What ideas have you taken to heart? What quotations have you valued? What have you found the most challenging? In this last day, take some time to reflect back. What qualities do you wish to develop on your lifelong spiritual journey? What precepts do you wish to continue to keep? What points about your spiritual journey are you still trying to understand? What practices do you wish to make a regular part of your life?

The art of reflection and remembering is a crucial part of living a spiritual life. It used to fascinate me that one of the major obstacles to meditation mentioned in the great Buddhist instruction manuals is simply "forgetting the instructions." So thinking back to what you learned and what you have experienced on the path is critical for continuing to build a strong foundation for a spiritual life. It helps us know what has been most helpful and what has not worked. It helps us reassess where we are in regard to our present circumstances.

There is an old Japanese story about a priest who challenged a Zen master to a debate. The priest was jealous of the Zen master and wanted to find a way to embarrass him in front of all his students. So he said, "The founder of my temple was so powerful and enlightened that he was able magically to transmit calligraphy through thin air. If he stood on one shore of a river holding a brush, and another person stood on the other shore holding paper, he could paint calligraphy in the air and cause an image to appear on the paper far on the other shore. Can you perform a miracle like that?"

The Zen master replied, "Perhaps your teacher performed that trick, but that is not the Great Way. My miracle is that when I feel hungry I eat, and when I feel thirsty I drink."

This story, like so many Zen parables, has several messages. One point of this story is that it is not what you do that matters but how you do it. The Zen master's life might not appear flashy. Enlightened living is not special, not miraculous, and not conspicuous. The Zen master's life consisted of simple and subtle everyday activity, done with mindfulness and wisdom.

Another point of this story is that dharma is doing what needs to be done. When you are hungry, eating needs to be done. When you are thirsty, drinking needs to be done. There is nothing wrong with knowing needs—your own and those of others—and finding ways to address them, not selfishly but simply. Dharma means finding the appropriate response to the call of the world and to life's demands.

To develop the ability to respond well to the world's demands, we have to train. There is another wonderful story from the biography of Milarepa that reminds us of the importance of the simple rigor of training. Milarepa had a close disciple named Gampopa. Gampopa spent some months studying and practicing meditation assiduously under Milarepa's strict guidance in a remote cave-community in Tibet. Finally, he was ready to return to his monastery. He knew, because of

Milarepa's age, that this might be their final good-bye. On the day of Gampopa's departure, Milarepa accompanied Gampopa down the trail leading away from the caves for some distance, holding his hand fondly. Then they said their good-byes, and Gampopa started down the mountain. Gampopa had walked quite a few yards when Milarepa shouted after him, "Wait!" Gampopa turned around, startled. Milarepa stood facing down the hill. "I have one final teaching for you!" Milarepa turned around and lifted his cotton robe. Milarepa's butt was covered in calluses from sitting on the hard stone cave floors for twelve years practicing meditation. Gampopa would later say he never got a more profound teaching.

To borrow the words of Seneca, the ancient Roman philosopher, "No one was ever wise by chance." We become wise by practicing. To practice means to do something repeatedly until you master it. Ideally, the exercises that I have included in this book will become the basis for your practice. After choosing the ones that appeal to you, make a reasonable commitment to regular practice, whether daily, every other day, or twice a week. You may want to take these exercises one by one and become proficient in each of them. If you are the kind of person who likes variety, you can rotate practices. If you like to go deep, focus on a single practice for a month or more before moving on.

As you have gathered, I believe all dharma practice comes down to deepening love and cultivating wisdom. With commitment and skill, that can be done under any circumstances. However, there are many avenues of support that you can seek out to nourish your spiritual work. I recommend that my students keep a spiritual or inspirational book by their bedside, then read slowly, just a page or passage at a time. Reading can itself be a practice.

I am a great believer in retreating. Most of my students sign up for at least one week-long meditation retreat every year. To find just the right group or place will take some research. Look on the Internet for retreat centers in your area, and find out what they offer. If you decide to do a solo retreat, be sure to rely on a meditation teacher (one with retreat experience) to guide you or give you instructions before you go off on your own.

Find a spiritual group in your community to practice with, if possible. This will also take some research, and you will probably have to visit several places until you find one you like. If you do not find such a place, commune with others who are also on a path (it does not need to be the same path!)—teachers, fellow seekers, and loving friends. The path cannot be traveled in isolation. The end of this book lists the Web sites of a few retreat centers that host a variety of spiritual teachers.

Finally, congratulations! Over the last seven weeks, you have probably tried on ways of thinking and being that are new and unfamiliar. You have communed with your own mind, the most incredible asset and the most troublesome companion you have. You have tasted your wisdom-nature. You have embarked on a journey that will challenge and change you.

In the beginning, I dedicated this book to the sage in you. At the end, I bow to her.

Exercise for Day Seven

Carrying Your Training on the Path

Target traits. List three target traits that you aspire to develop in the next year (examples: patience, being less judgmental, tolerance, warmth, fearlessness):

1. _____

2. _____

3. _____

Week Seven

Life practices. Go through *Everyday Dharma* and highlight/circle a few key practices that you plan to continue. Think about how you will do this. Daily? Several times a week? Write out your practice plan/schedule on your calendar or below.

_____

_____

_____

_____

_____

Precepts. Do you want to keep precepts? What will these look like? Write your moral imperatives below:

For (state time frame, such as "From now on;" "Until the end of the year;" "This month"):

_____

I will (write your precepts here):

_____

_____

_____

_____

Quotations. Go through *Everyday Dharma* and highlight the quotations that intrigue, interest, or inspire you. Copy or cut them out and post them where you can see them—not all at once, but so that you can focus on a quotation a week or a quotation a month.

Unanswered questions. What questions and experiences are you wondering about? What is still enigmatic and mysterious to you?
My unanswered questions:

_____

_____

_____

_____

_____

May you know every step of the path is the destination and every unanswered question is a good companion. May you find joy and enthusiasm on your journey.
May you be eager to meet the unexpected.
Most of all, each and every day, may you recognize your deepest nature, face to face.

Resources for Further Exploration

Reading books, exploring Web sites, and attending group events are good ways to learn more about Buddhism. Below are some lists to get you started.

DIGITAL SUPPORT FOR YOUR SEVEN-WEEK COURSE ON EVERYDAY DHARMA

Everyday Dharma's Facebook Group

www.facebook.com/home.php?ref=home#/group.php?gid=66456785488
Use this page to network with other people reading *Everyday Dharma*. Find a dharma buddy to go through the seven-week course at the same time as you do.

iTunes Podcasts

Download free iTunes podcasts of guided meditations found in *Everyday Dharma* by searching for "Lama Willa" on iTunes and subscribing.

Everyday Dharma Twitter Feed

Follow *Everyday Dharma* on Twitter: twitter.com/everydaydharma.

A SELECTION OF BUDDHIST SOURCE TEXTS

There are hundreds of Buddhist texts in translation, and many of them are good resources. Here are a few of my favorite source texts for inspirational passages and useful practices:

The Great Path of Awakening: The Classic Guide to Using the Mahayana Buddhist Slogans to Tame the Mind and Awaken the Heart, by Jamgon Kongtrul. This book lays out the traditional path of "mind training" as taught by the eleventh-century Buddhist monk Atisha. It contains practical advice for how to develop compassion and selflessness in daily activities.

The Debate of King Milinda, edited by Bhikkhu Pesala. This is a classic Buddhist sutra in which an Indian king meets the Buddha and asks him some tough questions. A good window into Buddhist philosophy.

Guide to the Bodhisattva's Way of Life, by Shantideva. A classic Buddhist text written by an eighth-century Indian scholar-monk. This book lays out the path of the bodhisattva, the Buddhist sage, in easy-to-remember verses. The chapters on anger and concentration are particularly powerful.

The Holy Teaching of Vimalakirti: A Mahayana Scripture, translated by Robert A. F. Thurman. A Mahayana sutra recording the dialogue between the wise man Vimalakirti and his students.

The Thirty-Seven Practices of Bodhisattvas, by Rgyal-Sras Thogs-Med Bzan-Po-Dpal. A classic Buddhist presentation, in thirty-seven verses, of the basic practices of the compassionate sage.

The Words of My Perfect Teacher, by Patrul Rinpoche. A commentary on the foundational practices of Tibetan Buddhism by a nineteenth-century Buddhist meditation master. Very readable and full of delightful traditional Buddhist stories told in a conversational style.

The Jewel Ornament of Liberation: The Wish-Fulfilling Gem of the Noble Teachings, by Gampopa. A classic text that lays out the basics of the Buddhist path from its beginning to its culmination, by a twelfth-century Tibetan Buddhist meditation master.

Clarifying the Natural State, by Dakpo Tashi Namgyal. A simple and direct meditation manual. This book focuses mainly on meditation practice.

The Life of Milarepa, translated by Lobsang P. Lhalungpa. A classic Buddhist biography of the yogi Milarepa, who lived in eleventh-century Tibet. A window into the Buddhist culture in Tibet.

Machig Labdrön and the Foundations of Chöd, by Jerome Edou. A classic Buddhist biography of the yogini Machig Labdrön, who lived in eleventh-century Tibet. A window into the life of Buddhist women in traditional Tibet.

SOME ONLINE RESOURCES

Natural Dharma (the organization that hosts most of Lama Willa's teachings), www.naturaldharma.org

Buddhanet (worldwide Buddhist information and education network), www.buddhanet.net

Dharmanet (Buddhist educational and informational resource), www.dharmanet.org

Tricycle: The Buddhist Review (resource for general information on Buddhism, especially Buddhism in America), www.tricycle.com

Access to Insight (searchable database of the Buddhist Pali Canon), www.accesstoinsight.org

Himalayan Art (searchable public database of Buddhist and Himalayan art from around the world), www.himalayanart.org

Quest Books (imprint of the Theosophical Publishing House, a source for books on spirituality, Gnosticism, Theosophy, and Buddhism), www.questbooks.net

Shambhala Publications (source for books on Buddhism and spirituality), www.shambhala.com

Snow Lion Publications (source for Buddhist books), www.snowlionpub.
com

Wisdom Publications (another source for Buddhist books), www.
wisdompubs.org

BUDDHIST MAGAZINES

Reading magazines is a great way to find out about current events, dharma gatherings, and retreats. It is also a good way to tap into the pulse of the American Buddhist world and the issues that affect it. Here is a selection:

- *Tricycle: The Buddhist Review*
- *Shambala Sun*
- *Dharma Life*
- *The Inquiring Mind*
- *Buddhadharma*
- *The Middle Way*
- *Turning Wheel*
- *Western Buddhist Review*

RETREAT CENTERS

There is nothing like having a full-immersion experience to deepen your practices of meditation and contemplation! While it takes a little planning, getting away for a weekend or a week to study with a Buddhist meditation teacher can be a transformative experience. Below are a few nondenominational retreat and city centers that offer introductory Buddhist programs (this list is not by any means exhaustive, but it gives you a place to start). You may also, in your Internet explorations, find a Buddhist monastery or retreat center near you that offers regular retreats.

Resources for Further Exploration

Omega Institute for Holistic Studies (Rhinebeck, NY, and other locations), www.eomega.org

Esalen (Big Sur, CA), www.esalen.org

New York Open Center (New York City), www.opencenter.org

Kripalu Center for Yoga and Health (Stockbridge, MA), www.kripalu.org

The Garrison Institute (Garrison, NY), www.garrisoninstitute.org

Kopan Monastery (Kathmandu, Nepal), www.kopan-monastery.com

The San Francisco Zen Center (San Francisco, CA), www.sfzc.org

Index

Index

Index

Index

Index

thoughts
  awareness of, 25
  in meditation, 29
  Thoreau on, 198
Three Arrivals meditation, 28–30,
  76, 112, 116
"three C's" of enthusiasm, 254
"three gates to liberation," 96
"three S's" (practices), 106–8
Tibetan Buddhism, 4–5, 60
Tilopa, 220, 262
timelessness, 108
traits, of heroes, 44–45
transcendence, 16
"treasure teachings," 202
Trisong Detsun, 201
Trungpa Rinpoche, 129
trust
  boundaries and, 207
  children and, 205–6
  power of, 204
  provisional and ultimate,
    209–13
  spiritual path and, 203–8
  three stages of, 211–13
truth
  as intuitive, 206
  as nondualistic, 260–61
  perspectives and, 244

U
unimpededness, 270–71
universal love. *See also* love
  as boundless, 136–41

  as compassionate, 144–45
  as fuel for spiritual journey, 123
  as impartial, 138–39
  as joyous, 146
  as moral imperative, 244
  as nonjudgmental, 142–43
  as selfless, 143–44

V
values, altruistic, 24
victory, giving to others,
  184–86
Vimalakirti, 260–61
visualization, 154–55
vows, 63

W
water
  as analogy for mind, 265
  as offering, 100
White Tara, 102–3
Whitman, Walt, 57
wholeness, 228
Winfrey, Oprah, 228
Winwood, Steve, 125
wisdom
  awareness and, 27–30, 265
  in heart, 3
  innate, 28, 264–66
  insight and, 260–62
  like ocean, 254
  primordial, 28
  as trait of sage, 105
Wisdom Moon, 67–68

Index

Quest Books

encourages open-minded inquiry into
world religions, philosophy, science, and the arts
in order to understand the wisdom of the ages,
respect the unity of all life, and help people explore
individual spiritual self-transformation.

Its publications are generously supported by
The Kern Foundation,
a trust committed to Theosophical education.

Quest Books is the imprint of
the Theosophical Publishing House,
a division of the Theosophical Society in America.
For information about programs, literature,
on-line study, membership benefits, and international centers,
see www.theosophical.org
or call 800-669-1571 or (outside the U.S.) 630-668-1571.

Related Titles

The Feminine Face of Buddhism, by Gill-Farrer-Halls
The Illustrated Encyclopedia of Buddhist Wisdom, by Gill Farrer-Halls
The Lost Teachings of Lama Govinda, edited by Richard Power
The Meditative Path, by John Cianciosi
Mother of the Buddhas, by Lex Hixon
The Opening of the Wisdom Eye, by H. H. the Dalai Lama, Tenzin Gyatso
Questions from the City, Answers from the Forest, by Ajahn Sumano Bhikkhu
A Still Forest Pool, by Jack Kornfield, with Paul Breiter
Tibetan Healing, by Peter Fenton
The World of the Dalai Lama, by Gill Farrer-Halls
The Zen of Listening, by Rebecca Z. Shafir

To order books or a complete Quest catalog,
Call 800-669-9425 or (outside the U.S.) 630-665-0130.